TEACHING
STUDY SKILLS

TEACHING STUDY SKILLS

Douglas Hamblin

BASIL BLACKWELL · PUBLISHER

First published in 1981 by
Basil Blackwell Publisher
108 Cowley Road
Oxford OX4 1JF
England

Reprinted 1982

British Library Cataloguing in Publication Data

Hamblin, Douglas
  Teaching study skills.
  1. Study, Method of
  I. Title
  371.3′028′14   LB1049

  ISBN 0 631 12533 7 Paperback
        0 631 12523 X Hardback

Typeset in VIP Bembo and Helvetica
by Preface Ltd., Salisbury
Printed and bound in Great Britain
at The Camelot Press, Southampton

Contents

Preface

This book incorporates much of the work on study skills I have undertaken in the last eight years. Thanks are due, and gladly given, to all my students who have helped me in so many ways. Next, I must acknowledge my debt to the many sixth form students with whom I have worked. My biggest debt is to those young men and women who came to see me regularly, sharing their inner doubts, aspirations, hopes and uncertainties in such an honest way. To them, I am especially grateful.

It is a great pleasure to thank Maggie Bradbury for her help in producing some of the diagrams. Frank Dickens has also generously allowed me to reproduce a little of the work we did together for a sixth form induction course. I am grateful to both of them. Edith Robinson deserves special mention, not only for her excellent typing, but for the way in which she maintained a vigilance which anticipated difficulties. It has, as usual, been good to work with her. Geoff Jones – an old friend – has given much support. He has the great gift of always being there when needed. To them all I offer my gratitude.

Swansea
November, 1980

Introduction

The purpose of this book is to show how pastoral care can help make the processes through which pupils learn, become part of a continuous dialogue between teacher and taught. The objective is that of reinforcing active approaches to learning. Truancy is frequently discussed today, yet the most insidious form of it – psychological truancy – is usually neglected. Pupils are present in the flesh, but absent in spirit. Lack of commitment and involvement in school work seems to be associated with passive and inert forms of learning. A programme of study skills designed to meet the needs of a school and administered methodically as part of tutorial work, is a partial corrective.

Behind the simple ideas presented in this book lies the assumption that effective pastoral care is complementary to curriculum development. That part of the pastoral effort, which pays attention to the processes through which pupils learn, is concerned with raising the level of performance of pupils. It should be an essential element in the school's attempt to attain its educational objectives. Study skills should be part of the structured programme of guidance which acts as the backbone of the pastoral effort.

Two types of study skills exist. First, there are the general skills which should be possessed by all pupils. These include, for example, the ability to read in a way which fosters recall of what has been read, and also generates new ideas; or the development of methods of note-taking which distinguish clearly between the salient and the peripheral. It is surprising how many students in the first year of the sixth form lack these skills, relying on copying from the blackboard or on the teacher's duplicated notes. Over-reliance on memorization is then inevitable, and they feel they are faced with a formidable task. Teachers who see the pastoral and curricular as inseparable recognize the links between poor study skills and stress or under-functioning. Too many pupils trap themselves into self-defeating cycles of frustration and feelings of inadequacy, becoming prisoners of their unprofitable modes of learning.

Next, the second category of study skills incorporates the principles of investigation which form the foundation of a particular discipline. They are therefore the sole responsibility of the subject specialist.

The reader may be tempted to say of the general study skills (which form the sub-structure on which the specialist skills rest), 'But we teach them already!' This would be to misunderstand the argument here, which is for the systematic – and consequently economical – incorporation into pastoral periods of activities which boost the pupil's sense of competence and of being in control. Haphazard and unmonitored approaches to this issue contain an unacceptable level of risk, in an age of economic uncertainty where achievement and initiative are vital for individual and national survival.

A central theme of this book is that study skills are not a set of procedures or recipes for action to be adopted unquestioningly. They *can* be presented in a mechanical way or with the authoritarian imperative, 'This is the right way to do it'. Such an approach might have immediate gains, but in the long run it would be doomed to failure, as it would reinforce stagnation and unthinking reactions to learning. More seriously, it also denies the individuality of the learner. The constructive teaching of study skills requires the presentation of many different activities. Pupils are then encouraged to experiment in an open-minded way, adopting the techniques which they find profitable.

No uniform pattern of study activity is imposed on the individual: he is helped to develop a style of learning which expresses his personality and meets his needs. This is because of the obvious fact that individuals have preferences and aptitudes which shape their learning. Some learn better through visual and diagrammatic methods, while others respond to verbal approaches. Limited opportunity for contact with pupils in our roles as subject teachers in the secondary school, restrict our opportunities to help pupils understand their preferences in study methods and integrate them into a productive learning style. Hence the importance of tutorial periods, especially where the tutor moves with his form for two or more years. By the time the student enters the sixth form, study skills should be taking the form of an inquiry into the modes of thought and methods of problem solving which produce competence for that person.

Attitudinal factors will also play a large part in the procedures outlined in subsequent chapters. As they pass through the secondary school, pupils strengthen their habitual responses to frustration, challenge and reward. Such behaviour patterns existed in earlier childhood, yet they assume shape and crystallize in middle and later adolescence. Teachers often comment on the negative changes in pupils' attitudes between the first and fourth years in the secondary school, without asking about the origins and functions of such attitudes. Some of the apathetic pupils may have a world view in which luck is unduly prominent. This may be the product of interaction in the classroom which suggests that the antecedents of success lie in the hands of others. The pupil then feels absolved from responsibility for his difficulties, and can blame others with a good conscience.

In recent years we have recognized the crucial contribution of the family to school success. Although the topic will not be dealt with directly, this discussion of study skills and achievement will focus on that which is learned within the family which impinges directly on school performance. Coping with the experience of frustration, anticipations of success or failure, or beliefs about the conditions for success, providing examples. In this way, the tutor can reduce the impact of unproductive attitudes, and modify behaviour to some extent, without resorting to attack or being reduced to blind exhortation. Both of those would be counter-productive.

The defensive stances mentioned in this introduction need to be examined openly. This should be done by the tutor, who has the best chance of developing essential relationships with the class. Obviously, headteachers have to give time, and the head of year or house has to give support and training to his tutors. We can ignore the possibility that the doubts and sense of vulnerability sometimes found at the onset of puberty, together with conflict engendered by crude and unskilled attempts at assertion, can contribute to study problems.

What can the tutor do? It is argued that part of the study skills programme is concerned with teaching students about the forces which influence performance for good or bad. Understanding them increases their sense of potency, and this feeling of mastery can be used to foster achievement. Let me illustrate: pupils can be trained to diagnose their learning difficulties, and then, in consultation with the form tutor, work out ways of improving performance. Responsibility is never removed from them.

Finally, two points must be made. Activities and ideas will be presented in each chapter. Readers should select what they need. If study skills are introduced later in the school – perhaps in the fourth year – then much of the earlier material can be used. The tutor must select what is germane to the needs of his form. This writer is not mistaken into thinking that there is any 'best way' or that unique insights have been acquired by him. All we have are methods, activities and sequences of presentation which only become effective when used selectively by those who know their pupils and the climate of the school. Next, the quality of the relationship between tutor and form is paramount. Not only does he implement the programme, but he has to help pupils understand themselves. Challenges have to be made without intimidation. Transfer of training has to be induced. We cannot assume that what has been learned in the form room will be used elsewhere – the old distinction between learning and performance is valid in the field of study skills. The tutor's relationship with his pupils provides the security necessary for intellectual independence and constructive endeavour. Without the supportive and accepting relationship, our attempts to foster positive approaches to learning will be abortive.

1: Study Skills and Achievement

WHAT IS THE FUNCTION OF THIS CHAPTER?

It shows why guidance for achievement should receive urgent consideration, and that it is a vital part of the task of the pastoral team. The skills which have to be fostered are outlined; and the reader should become aware that the approach suggested is constructively and creatively related to the central task of the school – the stimulation of active striving to attain standards of excellence. Every pupil, whatever his aptitudes and background, has the right to do something well. This can be accomplished, at least to a large degree, by the inclusion of carefully selected experiences in tutorial periods which reinforce the pupil's sense of mastery and strengthen his desire to be competent, by helping him develop a learning style which reflects his personality and interests.

There is no attempt to offer a recipe, or suggest that there is one right way of developing study skills. The teacher, as a professional, will select from what is presented and adapt it to meet the needs of his pupils. The objectives of the chapter are:

1 To show why guidance for achievement is an essential part of the pastoral task of the comprehensive school.
2 To explore the connections between study skills and achievement.
3 To consider the perceptual and attitudinal factors which either facilitate or impede effective learning.
4 To demonstrate the need for techniques of guidance which foster active approaches to learning and assist the development of independent study as preparation for higher and further education.
5 To outline the main skills that have to be developed.

WHY SHOULD WE INTRODUCE STUDY SKILLS AND GUIDANCE FOR ACHIEVEMENT IN THE PASTORAL PROGRAMME?

This is part of a positive response by the comprehensive school to the changing needs of society and the increased demands made upon teachers. This does not mean that we abdicate our professional responsibilities, or have to negate our values. Yet we have to adapt to an age where the future becomes increasingly difficult to forecast, and pupils need to be better equipped for survival than ever before.

In an age of economic uncertainty, it seems inevitable that the function of the comprehensive school in preparing pupils for life becomes the object of evaluation by many interested parties outside the school. Disquiet has, for example, been expressed by industrialists about the educational standards of entrants, and their ability to adapt realistically to the demands of the transition from school to work. The position is complicated by the need to prepare young people for the experience of enforced leisure and the removal of the basic structuring provided by regular work, as we experience a world recession and a move towards a post-industrial society.

It is difficult to say now how the changed economic situation will influence pupils' perceptions of the worth of school work. Legitimacy for the demands of the school for intellectual effort has been derived partially from its value as an admission ticket to a career. Many teachers report confusion in their pupils about the advisability of investing effort in gaining qualifications. Pupils are disinclined to obtain A-levels when they feel that the outcome may be unemployment.

The situation is, however, an open one. This writer and his students undertook a very recent study of 260 pupils in the fifth years of nine comprehensive schools as a first step in devising a programme of guidance to prepare pupils for the experience of unemployment. Open-ended questionnaires were used to eliminate the possibility of undue shaping of opinions by forced selection of responses. The responses were analysed by a group of teachers trained in pastoral care and guidance. The following may be illuminating:

1. When asked what advice they would give to a friend who had no job after leaving school:

24 per cent would suggest he kept looking for a job;

23 per cent would suggest he obtained further educational quali-
fication through the Further Education Colleges;

18 per cent would advise him to do voluntary social and community work;

13 per cent think he should pursue a hobby or sport;

2 per cent gave no answer or unclassifiable responses.

2. As mentioned above, the traditional legitimacy of schoolwork is problematical in current circumstances. The sample were
asked what advice they would give to someone who was thinking
about staying on at school, but who was not sure whether it was
the right thing to do. The results related to the relevance of education were:

46 per cent would advise staying on and getting further qualifications;

14 per cent would impress on them the difficulty caused by
leaving school without a job;

8 per cent would warn that there were few jobs available;

5 per cent would tell him to wait for his examination results.

3. When asked to state whether they thought schoolwork was
more or less important as jobs became harder to obtain:

94 per cent endorsed schoolwork as becoming more important;

2 per cent said they thought it would be less important;

4 per cent did not reply.

The reasons for endorsement of schoolwork becoming more
important as unemployment increases are interesting, especially
when we remember that the pupils provided them entirely without any restrictive list of possibilities being foisted on them.

18 per cent said jobs are becoming scarce (apparently they
linked this with the need to work in school);

18 per cent said it would give them more chance than others;

13 per cent stressed that especially good academic results would
help;

8 per cent saw it as important because it reflected the fact that
the person was willing to work;

5 per cent said the educated person was more worthwhile as a
worker;

20 per cent gave responses which contained a number of reasons
or which could not be coded under a broad heading;

8 per cent did not reply.

Even the slight evidence of these responses may serve to warn
us against early closure on a complex problem. The need to equip
adolescents to use their aptitudes and skills and gain a sense of

mastery may be increased rather than reduced by current circumstances. Study skills and guidance for achievement may have
increased importance in an age of ambiguous opportunity. Obviously, it will be only one facet of the approach to the problem. Let
the fifth year pupils speak for themselves in two more items taken
from the introductory study quoted above.

In view of the serious reactions found by social workers at
Corby after redundancies and unemployment, it was felt useful to
ask them to respond to this statement:

'Sometimes young people who are unemployed get fed up and
angry. What do you think they are likely to do when this
occurs?'

42 per cent felt that they would turn to vandalism and crime;
22 per cent felt they would become despondent and give up
looking for jobs;
6 per cent felt they would take it out on others;
6 per cent felt that the unemployed would turn to drink or
drugs;
3 per cent felt they would try harder to get a job;
3 per cent anticipated a suicide attempt;
6 per cent gave idiosyncratic answers which were not classi-
fiable, although relevant;
12 per cent made no response.

We may, in fact, be moving into a period when there will be a
need for higher achievement, and perhaps more surprisingly, for
attitudes conducive to the development of entrepreneurial skills in
the unemployed. Flexibility of thought, the ability to discard traditional conceptual frameworks, complexity of communication and
sophisticated management, may well be the hallmarks of post-
industrial development. Yet change inevitably brings a search for
scapegoats who can divest society of blame. This has been seen in
the claim that standards are falling in our schools. No lengthy
attempt to refute current complaints will be made, as this would
obscure the fundamental point that we may need to develop
higher standards of achievement than ever before as a matter of
survival.

But something must be said in our defence. Teachers are aware
that many young people now stay on at school who would have
left at the statutory leaving age twenty-five years ago. This is not
just a reaction to unemployment. It is partially an artifact of the

ever increasing demand for formal qualifications. Entry to a course of training as a State Registered Nurse now requires a minimum of five O-Levels, and many careers in commerce such as accountancy ask the potential entrant for A-Levels. It is likely that O-Levels are now being demanded for jobs where they are of little, if any, relevance.

We can also see that comparisons of the current performance of entrants with those of the past may be fallacious, because like is not being compared with like. A greater proportion of school leavers now proceed to some form of tertiary education; hence industry even today may still be receiving entrants who differ significantly in intellectual calibre. A dilemma is created for schools who have to meet the demand for increased qualifications from industry, and also equip more pupils for further education whilst coping with the implications of unemployment. It is this which makes the concept of guidance for achievement crucial despite current ambiguities and doubts. Equally important is the use of appropriate study skills which overcome the concealed underfunctioning of some able pupils. Their performance, although appearing to be satisfactory, is often below that of which they are capable.

Raising the level of achievement

The points made above do not imply a passive adaptation to contemporary pressures. Pastoral care has sometimes been conceived as diluted social work or as emotional first aid. Yet, although we have a pastoral function as teachers, our prime responsibility is to provide pupils with meaningful forms of success, recognizing the strength of Ford's (1969) statement that, for equality of opportunity, children from intellectually, socially and emotionally impoverished backgrounds need not the *same* education but *better* education. This is not rejecting pastoral care, merely recognizing that it is concerned with the achievement of the educational objectives of the school.

This book is therefore based on the belief that carefully devised programmes of guidance which provide a wide range of skills of study, and also modify the perceptions and attitudes related to achievement, not only have a compensatory function for some pupils but are *one* element in the basic task of creating a learning environment conducive to maximum achievement by every pupil. It would be short sighted for the school to over-emphasize the compensatory nature of the programmes, for access to study methods is not the prerogative of the disadvantaged. Pupils from materially good homes may have restricted forms of learning which limit the use they make of school experiences.

What support for guidance for achievement exists? The work of Bloom (1976) provokes thought. He argues (on the basis of experimental evidence) that individual differences in school learning will approach vanishing point under very favourable conditions, while with unfavourable circumstances they will increase with the passage of each year. In his analysis, he highlights the cognitive and attitudinal characteristics which the pupil brings to the learning task. Modification of the negative aspects and encouragement of positive development in these areas is, of course, at the heart of guidance for achievement.

Bloom is helpful because he makes a crucial distinction between individual differences in the *learner* and individual differences in *learning*. He argues that to concentrate on the learner's innate qualities, rather than his possession of relevant skills and knowledge, is esoteric and obscurant. The specific attitudes and skills necessary for a particular learning task are likely to be amenable to influence at most stages in the pupil's secondary school career. It is hard to deny that Bloom and his associates have demonstrated the strong possibility that, if slow learners were to be provided with consistently favourable learning conditions, they would become very similar to other pupils. We are then left with the problem of applying these positive findings to the British comprehensive school.

The argument in this book is analagous to Bloom's: provision of appropriate learning skills is vital if pupils are to use their talents to the full. In 1966 Parker and Rubin suggested that neglect of the processes through which pupils learned was a predominant feature of earlier attempts at curriculum development. Since then we have seen a shift of emphasis away from passive to active modes of acquiring knowledge, and recognition of the need to ensure that pupils apply newly-acquired information in a number of contexts. The importance attached to transfer of knowledge and training in this insistence upon application is welcome; yet we may still have failed to appreciate the handicaps of some pupils which stem from the lack of general skills of study. Doubts which have been expressed about the viability of modern methods of teaching (e.g. Bennett, 1976) may mean that these methods are less productive than they could be, because pupils have not been given the skills of active study in a systematic way. Teachers may assume that the skills are an incidental or an emergent product. Bloom argues for the careful analysis of specific learning tasks and the methodical preparation of pupils, so that they achieve success on the essential first steps of a task. This is vital, but there also is a place for the planned development of the general skills of study from which pupils select what is relevant to a particular task. Bloom's work emphasizes the provision of feedback to the learner in the early stages of a new task, and this is equally relevant to study skills. The tutor must ensure that helpful advice and evaluation is given. Hence study skills are developed through regular training in tutor periods, with the head of year or house guiding the process.

Post-industrial society seems to be demanding more of both teacher and pupil. The demands for evaluation of our effectiveness become increasingly vital. Therefore we cannot take the risk of assuming unquestioningly that pupils are acquiring the basic skills of study. The claim that each teacher is inculcating them cannot be accepted without query – for in practice, some appear to be doing this and others are not. It is often a haphazard process. Considerations of efficiency suggest that the staff of the school have to ask, 'What is the most economical and effective way of ensuring that all pupils are developing competent approaches to learning?' A survey of any comprehensive school would reveal pupils who have negative attitudes towards schoolwork because they predict and actually experience failure. They will not be confined to the less able, for we all know able pupils who underfunction, and who are also conveying less than positive perceptions of learning to other pupils. We sometimes restrict our explanations to attitudinal ones, failing to see the contribution of deficits in study skills or undue rigidity in using those which they possess.

Pastoral care incorporates the objectives of helping the school attain its educational goals, supporting the subject teaching, monitoring the pupil's progress and raising his level of aspiration. Therefore it is sensible to suggest that one component of pastoral care – which itself should be a structured process of continuous guidance – is a planned programme of activities designed to help pupils become competent learners.

THE IMPORTANCE OF OBJECTIVES

If this programme is to be a reality, then the pastoral team must have clear objectives. Statements of long term goals are grossly inadequate by themselves. Those responsible for a particular year must be able to itemize the skills of learning to which attention will be paid; they must be able to specify the ways in which the skills will be promoted; state the modifications which will be made for different groups of pupils, showing why this is necessary; lastly, they must be able to explain the relationship of the selected skills to current and future demands on pupils. Equally, what is taught in one year must be a logical outcome of what has gone before. Those responsible for pastoral care sometimes appear reluctant to commit themselves to an orderly progression as a prerequisite for the acquisition of study and social skills. It is important to note, therefore, that guidance for achievement is based – at least partially – on a sequential programme.

The importance given above to objectives and logical sequence does not imply the imposition of an uniform style of learning upon pupils. To attempt this would be to deny reality and doom the attempt at guidance for achievement to failure. Pupils have very different ways of perceiving and organizing their perceptions; therefore they must be given the opportunity to develop a style of learning and study which is meaningful to them. No blind attempt at offering a panacea is behind this book, nor is the professional responsibility of the teacher eroded. The guidance programme will contain experiences and activities from which individuals are encouraged to select what is meaningful to them, building up a resourceful and potentially creative approach to learning. To achieve this, part of the form tutor's activity will be the establishment of regular discussions about development in learning. Counselling as an activity stresses the need for self-awareness. Yet we may fail to see that in the school, discovery of the mode of thinking which yields results, translates intuitions into validated ideas, and allows one not only to analyse a problem but find imaginative solutions for it, may be the most valuable form of self-knowledge that we can give our pupils. Obviously, the inclusion of such self-discovery allows us to avoid a mechanistic and sterile approach to study skills. As a profession we may tend to ignore the fact that our expertise is not confined to the content of the subjects we teach. Indeed, it is more cogently seen as utilization of the processes through which people learn.

WHAT ARE WE TRYING TO ACHIEVE?

Our objective is the reinforcement of active learning. All too often in the secondary school, children conceive of learning as an alien activity, a ritual performance, that contributes little that is positive to their identity. They are reactive in the field of learning rather than proactive. It becomes 'something done to them' rather than an enjoyable and challenging enterprise. In my guidance work I find that pupils' complaints of 'being picked on in class' disappear as they take control of their learning.

To overcome inertia and apathy we need to back study techniques by experiences which help pupils appreciate that they are responsible for their own successes and failures – and that achievement is not dependent upon a capricious fate. It is the sense of being in control of one's destiny which, as Phares (1976) suggests, is associated with expectations of success. Exaggeration of the influence of a single factor on achievement would be naïve, if not foolish, yet experience shows that a widely-based programme of study skills can overcome the sense of drift and the depressed performance which are the usual concomitants of predictions of failure. Guidance for achievement should be preventive rather than remedial, and this, in conjunction with the objective of stimulating the desire to strive for excellence, demands that we reinforce the positive in our pupils and build up their self-esteem. Without self-respect there is unlikely to be *responsible* behaviour in the true sense of the word. The methods of teaching and the educational organization of the school are crucial. Yet, whatever the methods, study skills are essential. Where there is close concordance between the programme of guidance and the demands of the teaching methods, pupils are likely to benefit correspondingly.

EXPLORATION AND MASTERY

We cannot consider guidance for achievement apart from our views of the nature of man. Put starkly, we have to choose between a view of man as almost passively shaped by forces – early childhood experiences, dependency upon rewards and punishments, family background – or as capable of achieving mastery of his environment, making an impact upon a malleable world. White (1959) has argued that human beings are basically motivated by an intrinsic need to deal effectively with their environment. In his view, the hallmark of humanity is an inbuilt tendency to explore the environment and to strive for mastery. To the degree that man does this, he is true to himself. If this is a valid perspective, our qualms about the passivity of pupils is justified.

The opposite viewpoint is illustrated by extreme behaviourists who claim that behaviour is best understood by looking at its consequences. Thoughts and feelings are the product of behaviour; perhaps, at best, they merely co-exist with it. This leads them to claim that man cannot be autonomous in any real sense, for he is the hapless creature of this history of rewards and punishment. Skinner (1971) appears to be claiming that to understand behaviour we concentrate on the behaviour and its setting, ignoring feelings and cognitions as causes.

Such considerations may appear remote from the topic. In fact they are at the heart of the endeavour to stimulate achievement. If pupils are the prisoners of their pasts or of their family backgrounds, does education often function to confirm these identities? Helping pupils reach a position of responsible autonomy is the avowed aim of many teachers, although if Skinner is correct such an aim is delusory − the equivalent of the abortive pastime of chasing a chimera. For to try to achieve autonomy by processes of conditioning would be an example of man's capacity for self-deception, for autonomy involves rational choices.

The fact that many adolescents are passive learners, and apparently unable to use the resources of the school, seems to support the pessimistic conclusion of the inevitability of determination by the environment. But is it not likely that the apparent absence of White's postulated striving for mastery springs from a lack of appropriate skills? Pupils who are inert in school actively strive for mastery elsewhere. Inability to master key tasks in certain subjects through lack of skills leads to avoidance, coupled with the restriction of exploratory and mastery behaviours to non-academic areas. This then becomes compounded with experiences of failure and shame into a negative view of the school. The possibility can be illuminated by a personal example. As a young teacher this writer was taught that pupils often did not learn to read because they were maladjusted. It took me some years to realize that this was an incomplete statement. They might well have developed those attitudes of fight and flight labelled as maladjusted because they had failed to develop a skill of great social significance. Obviously, we shall have to take into account this reciprocity between study skills, attitudes and performance as part of the pastoral task.

WHAT TYPES OF STUDY SKILLS ARE INVOLVED?

In the introduction we recognized the importance of the specialist skills inherent in the structure and mode of thinking of a particular discipline which can only be fully comprehended by the expert in that field. It would be pretentious for the pastoral team to tamper with them.

The suggestions and activities provided will form the substructure (which includes the perceptual and attitudinal elements which either facilitate or retard positive responses to teaching) on which the specialist skills of a discipline can rest. It is now necessary to return to transfer of training. The importance of this cannot be overstressed. Conscious attention has to be given to the application of the study skills taught in the guidance sessions. Their relevance in classroom situations, homework or in examinations must be brought to the fore and the point hammered home. When one is concerned with general skills, to take for granted the fact that they will be transferred from the setting in which they are taught in other areas, is to court failure. Even the best experiences lose some of their impact when the teacher underplays their relevance. Study skills and achievement motivation are areas in which reliance solely upon pupils' self-discovery of their relevance is too great a level of risk.

The guidance programme has a compensatory function for some pupils, but older and abler pupils need it just as badly. Attention to the development of inferential thought, evaluation of the assumptions embedded in an argument, and questioning of the validity of evidence eventually bring rewards for teacher and taught.

The less able may need to be given the skills of tackling work in a structured and ordered manner, ways of dealing with homework assignments economically, and presenting work in a competent and attractive manner, as part of tutorial work. They may lack the skills of planning ahead, failing to see the relevance of earlier learning to that which comes later. Their methods of attack on problems or assignments may be ineffective, yet they appear unable to modify them, ignoring the signals that change is necessary for success. Enough has been said to indicate the type of general skills that are included, and the need to adapt to the pupil's strengths and shortcomings.

A guidance programme implies interruption of habitual patterns of response to learning tasks. To do this without causing anxiety or resentment is no easy task at times. But it cannot be evaded. Rigidity is frequently a source of underfunctioning, particularly in the conscientious individual who also seems vulnerable to anxiety. Without study skills, they carry on with unthinking approaches, sometimes reaching near desperation in the fifth year, when they exclaim just before the examinations, 'I'm working four hours a night, but I'm not getting anywhere!' Pupils like this cannot see that they should evaluate their study methods, acquiring skills which release them from over-reliance upon blind forms of memorization. Such pupils will always exist. They are likely to be detected in the first year of the comprehensive school when study skills are introduced as a matter of course. Both school and pupils benefit when the form tutor gains the skill of detecting pupils who are at risk, and exercises his duty of monitoring the progress of pupils in a way which takes him beyond mere exhortation and encouragement.

IS THE PROGRAMME CONFINED TO THE MECHANICS OF STUDY?

I have drawn attention elsewhere (Hamblin, 1978) to the processes which shape the picture the pupil holds of himself as a learner. Perceptions largely determine behaviour in learning situations. Man's capacity to represent his world is not without cost, for he who sees the world in negative terms is likely to experience it that way. Each one of us is largely responsible for what befalls him. It is strange that guidance has often avoided consideration of the cost to the pupil of holding a world view which gives predominance to luck and chance, restricting their sense of responsibility for what befalls them. Awareness of this can sometimes energize the previously passive boy or girl. Some pupils achieve a precarious freedom from overt anxiety about achievement by unduly limiting their aims and restricting their experience to what is familiar and safe. Unhappily, this evasion itself leads to a loss of self-respect which further erodes the motivation to learn, most probably by strengthening the tendency to predict failure as the eventual outcome. This is not inevitable, for as Thomas (1973) states in his review, the link between the self-concept and measures of attainment is complex and variable.

A pastoral team without knowledge of current work on achievement motivation is ill equipped to deal with guidance for success. Covington and Beery (1976) claim from experimental evidence that the pupil with a high need for achievement responds to failure when he experiences it by ascribing it to lack of effort or unsuitable study methods. He believes it was his fault, and consequently that he can correct the situation. A failure is therefore not seen as final, or as evidence that he attempted a task for which he did not possess the ability. Atkinson and Feather (1966) and Atkinson and Raynor (1974) discriminate between two fundamentally different types of achievement motivation: first, the active pursuit of success which is associated with positive predictions and the belief that the responsibility for success belongs primarily to the learner; second, the achievement activity intended to avoid either the humiliation produced by failure or criticism from authority figures in the pupil's life. This fear of failure produces unsatisfactory learning and perpetuates undue dependence on external surveillance.

There is another complication. Patty and Safford (1977) demonstrated the existence of the motivation to *avoid* success in some females. Success can be intimidating for them, because it brings them punishments of a subtle and indirect type. Those aspects of socialization which convey the likelihood that the successful female will, at best, be regarded somewhat doubtfully by males, are still surprisingly strong. Changes in this basic orientation toward achievement in females are still occurring, but the aspirations of girls are often low in relation to their ability, and contaminated by conflict between a compulsive image of femininity and the desire to use their talents to the full. Such issues assume prominence at the choice of A-Levels and in the decisions about the courses of further education they will follow.

For both boys and girls we shall have to include an analysis of the ways in which they cope with anxiety, resort to mechanisms of avoidance or falsely bolster their beliefs about the nature of achievement. Strategies of guidance will include self-diagnosis of difficulties, application of the principles of target-setting and the use of friends as a source of help.

THE IMPORTANCE OF PEERS

Teachers are keenly aware of the way in which the peer group as a force inhibits performance. The group can impose a norm of mediocrity or punish those who wish to excel. Pupils are unduly susceptible to taunts of 'creep' or 'teacher's pet'. The same tendencies can be found in their reactions to the invitation to play truant or indulge in disruptive behaviour. 'Saving face' is one of the mechanisms that guidance for achievement has to take into account. A constructive attack on this should begin in the first year, and second year guidance should concentrate on it and on sources of frustration which arouse defensive strategies in pupils.

Adolescents can hold partial and distorted conceptions of learning, and of the motivation and intentions of teachers, which they strengthen among themselves. Although we are aware that peers and the peer culture have a stronger influence over the values, attitudes and behaviour of young people than the school, over-estimation of the peer group as an influence is self-defeating. It is still a force to be reckoned with, as Kandel and Lesser (1972) revealed in their study. But they also showed that in some decisions and problems adolescents refer to their parents, while with others friends are the prime source of support. We can be in implicit collusion with low performance when we attribute to the peer group more power than it possesses.

From the perspective of guidance for achievement it seems judicious to enlist the potential opposition as a help in developing standards of excellence and raising attainment instead of merely regretting its capacity for inhibiting our influence. Vorrath and Brendtro (1974) are only two among a number of writers who have shown the success that is derived when peer support is used to treat delinquency. Goodman (1972) has shown that informal and largely untrained helpers can be as effective as professionals. Similarly, Guerney (1969) makes the same point, drawing evidence from a number of fields. This evidence of the value of peer support alerts us to the possibility that we are ignoring one of the most potent sources of support, the mobilization of which would benefit everyone within the school. Emphasis on active forms of learning, and acceptance by the pupil of his own accountability for success or failure, almost impel us to include peer support as an integral and major part of the programme. Friends can help, stimulate and reward one another when our surveillance is removed.

WHAT SKILLS HAVE TO BE DEVELOPED?

Activity replacing passivity and avoidance is the basic theme in this approach to guidance for achievement. This is built into the ten areas of skill set out below in ways related to the age, ability and background of the pupil:

1 *Listening*: this will be treated in a way which links it with recall.
2 *Reading*: the mechanics as well as recall and the development of inferences will receive attention. Reading as a way of generating new ideas will be stressed.
3 *Presentation of work*: this is a skill which is often disregarded

or has not been developed by pupils. Yet it is closely associated with competence and the growth of respect for oneself
as a learner.

4 *Active methods of homework*: consistent training in homework
  methods is necessary if negative attitudes are not to develop.
  Pupils not only underfunction in school, but in their
  homework.
5 *Planning and target setting*: a key skill in which peer support
  will be essential.
6 *Essay writing and answering questions*: continuous attention
  has to be paid to these skills if pupils and teachers are to
  benefit from their hard work.
7 *Revision and examination techniques*: an area which will be
  treated in different ways at different ages, but one which
  progressively becomes more important.
8 *Note-taking*: an area of weakness.
9 *Raising the level of aspiration and inculcating the motive to succeed*: vital, yet an area which is rarely dealt with systematically.
10 *Evaluation*: a skill which is not the prerogative of the
  teacher: pupils must be taught to evaluate their own work.

The phrase 'age, aptitudes and backgrounds' reverberates with
overtones of ideals which have long been cherished in education.
Ideals are not romantic or unrealistic. A guidance programme
which embodies positive discrimination or forms of adaptation to
the cognitive functioning of pupils can help translate ideal into
reality. The less able need to extend their repertoire of learning
behaviours. Their impoverished and monotonous world is
reflected in a corresponding limitation in the tools they possess
with which to tackle the task of learning.

Many pupils possess intelligence they cannot use because they
react blindly, treating different situations as if they were identical.
Verbal labels or simple formulae for behaviour are applied to people and tasks in inappropriate ways. Problems which need different orientations and methods are approached in a habitual way
which takes no cognizance of variations in structure or basic conditions, because their pupils' powers of discrimination are poorly
developed. The end result is that they hold a conception of learning mainly phrased in terms of memorization and the regurgitation of largely uncomprehended facts. Predominance is given to
their negative attitudes in discussions, but we fail to see that such
attitudes are effect rather than cause in many cases – the product of

inability to cope, through lack of skills. After some years of inability to cope they seek compensations elsewhere, escaping or trying to avoid a classroom situation which they see as either irrelevant or noxious. They then reject the whole learning process as threatening and unrewarding. If the pastoral team then stress home background and personality, ignoring basic learning skills, little is likely to change. Explanation of failure in learning in terms of family and innate factors without reference to skills and the classroom situation is, at the best, likely to be incomplete.

The problems of the disadvantaged may preoccupy us, so we may assume too lightly that the able pupil does not have problems of study. Yet Jacobs (1974) found that sixth form pupils had inadequate study skills. For such pupils, the programme will develop awareness of the advantages and disadvantages of their style of thought, for above a certain threshold of intelligence performance is largely determined by this. Messick (1976) has defined cognitive style as the stable preferences, attitudes or habitual strategies which shape a person's typical mode of perceiving and thinking. This underlies this writer's (Hamblin, 1978) contention that his style of thought and problem-solving is as legitimate an object of enquiry for the sixth form student as is the content of the subject he is studying.

Questions must be raised about the selection and processing of information, and the development of the ability to work within the constraints of a set problem without ignoring those constraints and coming to a false conclusion. Equally crucial is the ability to discard the frame of reference when necessary and look at what is possible rather than just at what exists. An interesting topic for investigation is that of susceptibility to social influence and the nature of the personality factors which impede some sixth form pupils when they try to restructure ideas into an original or different framework. Some idea of the content of the guidance sessions can be gained if we see that it is important to examine the forces in communication which lead to over-simplification and the denial of relevant differences. Just as important would be the tendency to concentrate on a few points in an argument, accentuating their importance. These, of course, are the equivalents of the processes of levelling and sharpening described in the psychology of rumour and perception.

Finally, we see that pupils have to be assisted to move towards the stage of independent learning and study. This, as Alexander and Burke (1972) argue, is more than study without direct supervision. It is learning which is motivated by the learner's own purposes, bringing him intrinsic rewards and satisfaction. Guidance for achievement helps free pupils from reliance upon external rewards, producing learners who engage in study on their own initiative without undue permission or coercion from others.

A FINAL NOTE

It will now be obvious that this book contains no ready-made prescriptions for practice. The reader will merely find ideas, techniques and activities from which he can select what fits the needs of pupils. The programme has to be tailored to fit the school and children. Even when this is done, pupils should be encouraged to select what is useful and relevant to them. Our objective in the pastoral programme is to provide experiences, allowing the pupil to discover if they are valid for him. Obviously, time is necessary for this, because skills are not acquired immediately, and some pupils take longer than others to assimilate them. Some pupils fear or deride the unfamiliar; others accept novelty uncritically, embracing it eagerly, only to discard it in a few weeks. This has to be prevented.

We are encouraging pupils to engage in a long-term process of building a style of learning which is meaningful and productive. Pastoral care embodies the ethic of profound respect for individuality. To try to impose a learning style is the pedagogic equivalent of imposing a false self upon someone – an act which is inevitably as destructive in the long run. To enhance the creativity of the comprehensive school, the pastoral team has to abandon limited conceptions of its functions – emotional first aid, modified forms of social work and 'getting to know the pupils' – for this wider view which subsumes them under the endeavour to provide guidance for achievement. A school which does not set out to provide guidance for achievement as an integral part of pastoral care is likely not only to have underfunctioning pupils, but to be an underfunctioning school.

2: The First Two Years

Guidance for success is both preventive and positive in the first two years of comprehensive schooling. It is preventive because it anticipates the development of negative attitudes towards learning, school, teachers and effort which appear in some pupils towards the end of the first year and during the second year. The full impact of these attitudes on behaviour may not become evident until the fourth or fifth years. Modification of disruptive and alienated behaviours then entails a heavy expenditure of time and effort, and the outcome is often disappointing.

Movement from primary education to secondary is a major transition which can severely test the pupils' powers of adaptation. Adams *et al.* (1976) describe clearly the stresses involved in the experience of transition. Inability to predict the outcomes and exposure to new demands can reveal the individual's inadequacies unless help is given. Coping with the unfamiliar certainly can lead to stress, but it can also stimulate. Let us be positive: entry to the comprehensive school can be invigorating and a spur to development because it gives the pupil a new start. He has an opportunity to break (if they exist) old links between school and failure. But the presence of new possibilities does not necessarily mean that pupils will take them without some help.

More important than the transition and the imposition of new demand is the demonstration by Yinger *et al.* (1977) that it is possible to reduce or even eliminate educational deficits through new and challenging experiences. Their programme was very different from the one advocated here and was based on a wider view of compensatory education in adolescence. Yet Yinger and his associates are able to show that a six week summer programme followed by a 'modest series of related activities' during the succeeding five years had a significant effect on academic achievement. It is at least likely therefore that a systematic and coordinated programme of guidance incorporating study skills will have a good effect on school performance. The rub comes in the words *systematic* and *co-ordinated*, for we are slow to learn that the price of success is continuous effort and guidance.

Great emphasis has been placed in education on the relationship of family and neighbourhood to attainment and acceptance of the ends of the school. This is necessary, but is insufficient of itself. Understanding of the influence of these wider factors helps us chart our paths to the goals and anticipate the hazards, but it does not provide the skills pupils need. Guidance in the first two years of the secondary school builds up a sense of potency and taps unused capacity by providing pupils with the skills of tackling homework successfully, reading efficiently and moving towards self-management in learning. Practical guidance is based on the belief that the most likely way of changing a pupil's response to school is to give him the tools he needs for success. This will then make it possible for him to change his interaction with teachers and view them positively.

WHAT SKILLS SHOULD WE DEVELOP?

Suggestions are made below. The sequence in which the items are presented makes no pretence of being an ideal one; it merely reflects what has been found to be useful. It is in no sense prescriptive. The year head or form tutor will usually select activities from a number of areas on the basis of his judgement of the needs of a particular form. Sometimes, there will be a need to concentrate in depth on an area in which deficits are creating problems, e.g. listening.

STUDY SKILLS IN THE FIRST TWO YEARS

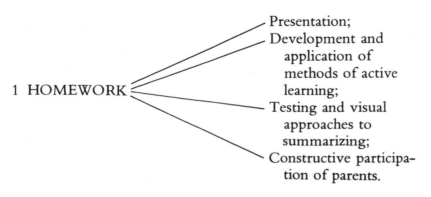

1 HOMEWORK
- Presentation;
- Development and application of methods of active learning;
- Testing and visual approaches to summarizing;
- Constructive participation of parents.

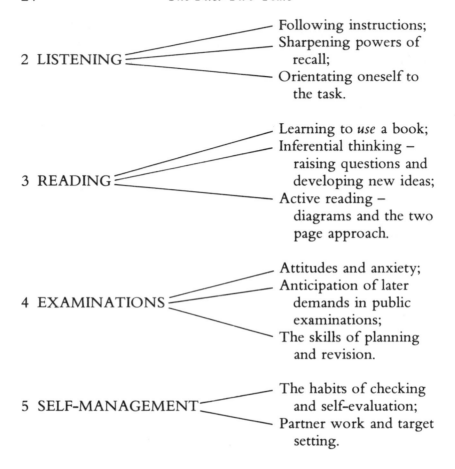

2 LISTENING
- Following instructions;
- Sharpening powers of recall;
- Orientating oneself to the task.

3 READING
- Learning to *use* a book;
- Inferential thinking – raising questions and developing new ideas;
- Active reading – diagrams and the two page approach.

4 EXAMINATIONS
- Attitudes and anxiety;
- Anticipation of later demands in public examinations;
- The skills of planning and revision.

5 SELF-MANAGEMENT
- The habits of checking and self-evaluation;
- Partner work and target setting.

Recipes and rigidity are both inappropriate. The activities should therefore incorporate clear objectives; give experiences which lead to the acquisition of skills; yet do not impose solutions in an inflexible manner on the individual. The idea of possible strategies and selection of what is meaningful for each pupil replaces the concept of a 'right way'. Active learning is probably best induced by participation in structured experiences which highlight a particular skill, illustrate its application and then allow a pupil to consider adopting it, adapting it or rejecting it after due thought.

The following framework if consistently used makes good use of time and translates the statements of intention above into reality.

A BASIC FRAMEWORK FOR THE GUIDANCE LESSON

1 A clear *statement of the objectives* of the activity which also stresses its relevance for the pupils. (1–2 minutes)
2 A carefully devised *activity* which is undertaken by groups of 2–4 pupils. (7–15 minutes)
3 A final phase in which the form tutor makes the learning *explicit* and *reinforces* it. Stress is given to the *immediate application* of what has been learned. (7–15 minutes)

This simple framework has the merit of allowing the form tutor a real opportunity to use his skills as a teacher in the tutorial period. Not only does it provide pupils with purposeful activity, but it requires the tutor to stimulate transfer of training. Without the tutor's follow-up and his work on applying the technique, the session is at best less effective than it could be. At the worst it degenerates into mere entertainment or time filling. Every scrap of the tutor's teaching skill is required if the conclusion of the period is to build on the experience. The better someone is as a teacher, the better they will be as a form tutor.

Other points have to be made. Many teachers are unused to dealing with small group activities as part of a lesson. Small groups can merely mean working with a partner. When groups of three or four pupils are required, pupils merely turn round. No disorder is necessary! Indeed, it is vital that the guidance sessions should have a clear framework and be conducted with a sense of vigour and purpose. If disorder occurs, then it will be profitable for the tutor to look at the way in which he moves from stage to stage or in which he introduces the session or ends it.

Classroom management has to be evaluated if the form tutor is to utilize fully the scarce resource of time. Routines are not to be despised as they are at the heart of good classroom management. I have often noted that the impact of a first rate guidance session conducted by an experienced tutor has been lessened because he or she had not developed an efficient system of distributing materials speedily. Thus momentum is lost, and precious time is spent in restoring interest which could have been maintained. When unwieldy methods of distributing materials are accompanied by unclear instructions, the tutor may find himself without sufficient time for his vital contribution at the end of the session. Without this, transfer of training – always a source of concern – becomes a chancy affair. The activity is then judged to be at fault, when in fact the failure is due to the tutor's inefficiency in organizing the session.

This, in conjunction with the lack of clear objectives, leads to pastoral care being contaminated by the theory of the impossible task. We feel that too much is being asked of us or that the resources at our disposal are deficient, and that we cannot attain our goals. Yet the structure set out above allows the form tutor to use even a brief period of 15 to 20 minutes productively. Provided (and this proviso emphasizes the needs in schools for heads of year and house who have training, management skills and the ability to develop materials) that the programme systematically tackles key areas and incorporates meaningful activities, one weekly period of guidance during the first five years in the comprehensive school can be of real help to pupils.

Details of activities follow. The form tutor may be apprehensive about constructing materials, or find the task intimidating. In fully-functioning pastoral systems the development of materials will be a team effort in which the heads of year or house play a major part. Economy of effort exists when the middle management figures realize they have to develop materials and phase tasks so that form tutors are not overwhelmed. Building a resource bank of materials is an essential part of their task. Once the materials are produced they are available in succeeding years, and in three or four years the range of activities available is surprising. Should the reader doubt this, let me quote the instance of a school with whose staff this writer worked on a training day some few years ago. All the staff (including the headmaster) worked on the development of materials. At the end of the day, they had built up a stock of ideas and activities which, although needing further refinement and actual production, would be sufficient to see them through their first year in developing a pastoral curriculum.

Finally, the suggestions are not exhaustive – they are merely illustrative. Each one can be developed by the capable form tutor. Indeed, I have seen variations of them by students which have been of great interest; the derivative was at least as good as the original. In the hands of an enthusiastic form tutor these basic ideas become highly creative.

HOMEWORK: CAN WE TEACH PUPILS AN ACTIVE APPROACH TO IT?

Attitudes towards homework reflect the pupil's general attitudes towards school. Accepting that homework is essential for academic success – admittedly a view which is not shared by every teacher – it seems curious that so little training aimed at the development of competence in this field is given to pupils. Counter-productive habits are unwittingly reinforced. Pupils often learn that homework can be given cursory attention; that it is an activity which is undertaken on the school bus or in a corner of the cloakroom; and perhaps that it consists of the inaccurate transfer to your own book of what your best friend has done. Homework is often at the heart of conflicts between pupils, parents and teachers, yet we do not always manage to involve parents constructively. Increasing importance is given to it as pupils reach the stage of public examinations, although this does not mean they are doing it well. Indeed, the cry, 'I'm working hard every night, but not getting anywhere!' is all too frequent. Prevention of this plight begins in the first year.

Presentation

Many pupils come into the secondary school with little, if any, experience of homework and therefore have not learned to present it attractively. In some homes, parents and older siblings offer pupils models of an orderly approach which they are rewarded for emulating. But this is not inevitable. The following package of activities allows the tutor to begin to foster pride in their work.

Activity 1
Objective: To create awareness of the basic elements of good homework.
Pupils are presented with several examples of attractive layout of homework exercises. These are photocopied and therefore look very like what the pupil could produce. Indentation, underlining, the use of capitals to make key words stand out, devices such as asterisks in the margins which identify main statements, can all be included (see Figs 1–3).

In this activity pupils compare the examples, discussing the merits of each with a partner and deciding which features they would like to adopt. Even at this stage, pupils are encouraged to make their own decisions and develop their own style of presentation. Imposition often destroys ego-involvement.

The final discussion should highlight the functions of such devices as underlining, capitals and asterisks in helping pupils distinguish between the salient and the marginal.

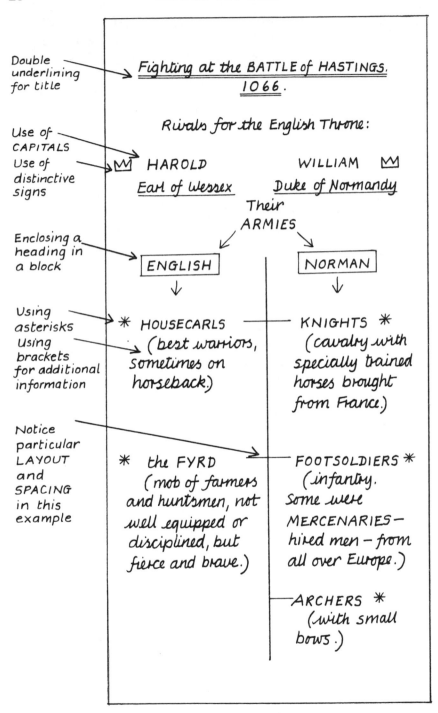

Double underlining for title

Use of CAPITALS
Use of distinctive signs

Enclosing a heading in a block

Using asterisks
Using brackets for additional information

Notice particular LAYOUT and SPACING in this example

Fighting at the BATTLE of HASTINGS. 1066.

Rivals for the English Throne:

HAROLD   WILLIAM
Earl of Wessex   Duke of Normandy

Their ARMIES

ENGLISH   NORMAN

* HOUSECARLS   KNIGHTS *
(best warriors, sometimes on horseback.)   (cavalry with specially trained horses brought from France.)

* the FYRD   FOOTSOLDIERS *
(mob of farmers and huntsmen, not well equipped or disciplined, but fierce and brave.)   (infantry. Some were MERCENARIES — hired men — from all over Europe.)

ARCHERS *
(with small bows.)

Figure 1

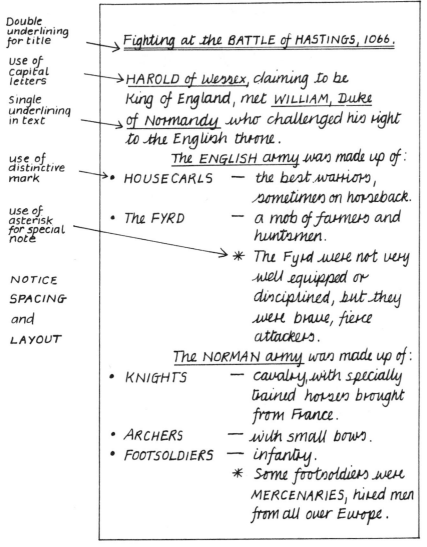

Double underlining for title →

Use of capital letters →

Single underlining in text →

use of distinctive mark →

use of asterisk for special note →

NOTICE

SPACING

and

LAYOUT

<u><u>Fighting at the BATTLE of HASTINGS, 1066.</u></u>

<u>HAROLD of Wessex</u>, claiming to be King of England, met <u>WILLIAM, Duke of Normandy</u> who challenged his right to the English throne.

The <u>ENGLISH army was made up of</u>:
- HOUSECARLS — the best warriors, sometimes on horseback.
- The FYRD — a mob of farmers and huntsmen.
    * The Fyrd were not very well equipped or disciplined, but they were brave, fierce attackers.

The <u>NORMAN army was made up of</u>:
- KNIGHTS — cavalry, with specially trained horses brought from France.
- ARCHERS — with small bows.
- FOOTSOLDIERS — infantry.
    * Some footsoldiers were MERCENARIES, hired men from all over Europe.

Figure 2

Activity 2
Objective: To help pupils take the standpoint of the teacher.
Two pieces of homework are presented to the pupils. As before, they are reproduced by spirit duplicator, but while one is neat, attractive and well organized, the other is messy and unattractive. Pupils then discuss in small groups of three of four how they think the teacher will judge these pieces of work, giving reasons for the teacher's judgement.

Fighting at the Battle of Hastings - 1066.

Harold of Wessex, claiming to be King of England, met William, Duke of Normandy, who challenged his right to the English throne.

* The ENGLISH army was made up of :-

A. HOUSECARLS

These were the best warriors, who were sometimes on horseback.

B. the FYRD

These were a mob of farmers and huntsmen. The Fyrd were not very well equipped or disciplined, but they were brave, fierce attackers.

* The NORMAN army was made up of :-

A. KNIGHTS

These were the cavalry troops, with specially trained horses brought from France.

B. ARCHERS

These were armed with small bows.

C. FOOTSOLDIERS

These were the infantry troops. Some footsoldiers were mercenaries, hired men recruited from all over Europe.

Figure 3

Many pupils lack the ability of standpoint-taking – the capacity to construct the role of the other in imagination and see things from their perspective. This activity encourages them to evaluate homework and also to see things through the eyes of the teacher.

The final discussion will stress the need to understand the way in which the teacher will judge work, why he does this and the need to anticipate his judgements in order to improve work. (This will lead to a later activity on self-evaluation of work.)

Activity 3
Objective: To teach pupils to make attractive diagrams.
Present the class with two different examples of homework (Figs 4 and 5). Both of them are reasonably set out as far as the written work is concerned. They contain the same diagram, but one is competent and has a neat heading, uses colour attractively, is enclosed in a box, and has no crossings out. The other is untidy and contains some obvious errors. Partners discuss the untidy diagram, comparing it with the other one, testing as many faults as they can find in three minutes.

They are then given seven to ten minutes to produce their own diagram, trying to improve on the good one if they can. They then compare diagrams with partners and discuss the merits of each.

The final contributions by the teacher will focus on the functions of diagrams in textbooks and in homework, showing their importance.

Activity 4
Objectives: (a) To introduce pupils to active evaluation of their own work; (b) To further reinforce awareness of the main elements of competent presentation.
From the first year of secondary schooling pupils should be encouraged to take an active part in the evaluation of their own work. This is helped by training them to apply periodically a self-checking schedule such as the one which is reproduced below. Most role specifications for the form tutor include some mention of periodic progress reviews. The self-assessment form involves pupils in the process, while the discussion which follows its use can alert the tutor to pupils who are at risk. They will include those who tend to be unduly self-condemning, as

DIAGRAM OF THE EAR

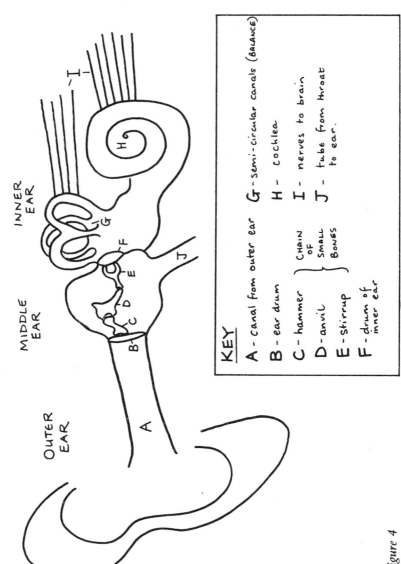

OUTER EAR

MIDDLE EAR

INNER EAR

KEY

A - canal from outer ear

B - ear drum

C - hammer ⎱ CHAIN
D - anvil ⎰ OF SMALL
E - stirrup   BONES

F - drum of inner ear

G - semi-circular canals (BALANCE)

H - cochlea

I - nerves to brain

J - tube from throat to ear.

Figure 4

Diagram of the ear

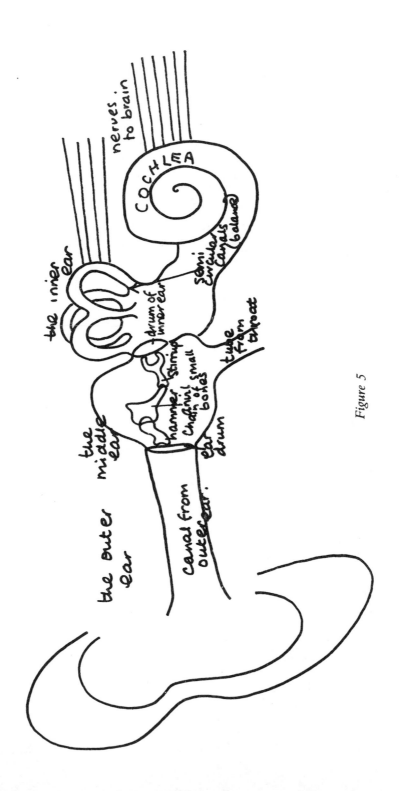

nerves.
to brain

COCHLEA

Semi
circular
canals
(balance)

the inner
ear

drum of
inner ear

the
middle
ear

Stirrup

Hammer!
Chain of small
bones

ear
drum

tube
from
throat

the outer
ear

Canal from
outer ear.

Figure 5

well as those who fail to appreciate the need for order and neatness.

Two other points should be made. The administration, discussion and use of a self-evaluation schedule is an early step towards the development of intrinsic motivation, i.e. working for internal rather than external rewards. Next, the final section on the setting of simple concrete targets for improvement is more important than it may seem, because it prepares pupils for later work on raising the level of aspiration. The form tutor should encourage the class to work on the section *Improving yourself*, and he should allow discussion in the next guidance period of whether or not the targets were achieved, rewarding any efforts with approval. He should concentrate on the positive achievements, bearing in mind that even in guidance activities it is possible (and self-defeating) to pay more attention to the behaviour of which we disapprove than that which we hope to induce.

LEARN TO CHECK UP ON YOURSELF
(A Self-Assessment Form for First and Second Year Pupils)

Why this form could be useful to you:
As you get older you will be expected to take responsibility for your work. The successful pupil is one who looks at his work and corrects mistakes. He also sets himself targets for improvement.

How to use the self-assessment form:
There are a number of ways of doing this. You can:
    a use it yourself to assess a piece of work and see how satisfied you are with it;
    b ask a friend to help you see how well you have done the work:
    c use it to decide what you will do to improve your performance.

The appearance of your work:
    1 Is it neat? ....
    2 Did you put the title? (if this was necessary) ....
    3 Did you have proper margins? ....
    4 Did you underline the title and other headlines carefully? .....
    5 Did you start each paragraph in the usual way? ....
    6 Any other ways in which you could improve the neatness of your work:
        ....
        ....

The important parts of your work:
1 Is your writing easy to read? ....
2 Did you check your spelling? ....
3 Have you checked the punctuation? ....
4 Would you say your diagrams or drawings were carefully done? ....
5 Have you corrected any mistakes? ....
6 Could you honestly say that you did your best ....

Improving yourself

There is not much point in saying 'I will work harder'. You must say HOW you will work harder.

State *exactly* what you will work extra hard on in your next piece of work. When you have done it, come back to this form and give yourself a mark for the improvement.
1 What I will improve in my next piece of work ....
....
2 How I will tackle it ....
....
3 My mark for my improvement:
Excellent   Very good   Good   Fairly good   Poor

_____   _____   _____   _____   _____

Activity 5

Objectives: (a) To help pupils increase their awareness of the attributes leading to competent learning and homework; (b) To begin to encourage them to discuss the requirements for success in schoolwork and begin to detect those which are crucial.

Before the class enters the tutor has attached colourful cards with adhesive tape to the blackboard which are large enough to be read by the pupils. Each card refers to a quality or skill contributing to good homework. The cards should number about 12–15 and might include:

     neatness; correct order; underlining; careful checking; accurate spelling; following instructions; testing yourself; handing in on time; regular time for homework; keeping a homework diary.

The form is divided into groups of 6–8 pupils. They are told:
    i an auction will take place;
    ii each group has £150 to spend to buy the qualities which they think are essential for success;
    iii each group must appoint a 'bidder' who will buy on their behalf;

iv once the bidding commences they can only communicate
by signs which indicate whether they wish him to desist
or raise the bid. If they communicate in any other way the
auctioneer will ignore their bid.

Pupils enjoy inventing their own signals, but shortage of time
may compel the tutor to tell them what to use.

Chairs have already been placed at the front of the class where
the groups can see their bidders. The tutor then becomes the
auctioneer selling each quality in turn, handing it over to the
'bidder' as it is 'knocked down'. At the end of the auction,
which is briskly conducted, the bidders return to their groups,
who then discuss questions posed by the tutor, e.g.:

i What other qualities would they have liked to purchase if
they had been given more money?

ii How satisfied are they with the qualities they have
bought?

iii Are there other qualities essential for successful
homework which they think should have been included in
the list?

Activity 6
*Objectives: (a) To help pupils learn to distinguish between central and
marginal elements in homework skills; (b) To stimulate the development of a personal hierarchy of learning skills as part of intellectual
development.*
The qualities – which can be similar to those given in Activity
5 – are written in a random way on one side of the blackboard.
On the other side a ladder is drawn with not   1
more than seven or eight steps. As 12–15 quali-   2
ties are written on the board, the group has to   3
select the best ones. The tutor then gets some   4
ideas from the form about the most important   5
quality and writes this in the space numbered 1   6
on the ladder. He then gets ideas about the next   7
most important quality and is apparently about   8
to write it in. In fact, he stops and suggests that some pupils may
not agree or that the class is merely 'pleasing teacher' by giving
him the answers they think he wants. Duplicated sheets containing the ladder and the list are handed out. Pupils then fill in
their individual ladders and then discuss the results in small
groups of three or four. They are encouraged to compare their
lists and justify their own rankings. The tutor then ends the

session with a vigorous group discussion which looks at the justifications for the rankings.

This activity, although simple, illustrates the style of thought behind guidance activities. Pupils are given support through the tutor's initiatory activity, but as soon as possible they proceed to work independently. The danger of stimulating socially desirable answers is in the tutor's mind, but he also communicates awareness of this to the pupils constructively. Many sixth form pupils confuse the skill of appraisal with the presentation of opinions unbacked by evidence or rational argument. Even in this first year activity, the tutor encourages pupils to be aware of the reasons for their choices, testing them out first with peers and then in the general discussion.

Activity 7
Objectives: (a) To consolidate previous learning about homework skills; (b) To give an experience which will reinforce feelings of competence.
The form is presented with a duplicated copy of an untidy piece of homework (Fig 6). The tutor has written key words on the blackboard which refer to the defects in the example, e.g. *margins, underlining, spelling*. Their attention is drawn to the fact that these words are clues. Brief partner discussion of the merits and faults of the piece of work then follows. The pupils then rewrite it, comparing efforts at the end.

In the final discussion the tutor reinforces the importance of evaluating one's work, and also praises the class for effort, positive attitudes and the application of skills they have learned in earlier sessions.

(This activity highlights another point. During the activities the tutor moves from group to group noting issues that are emerging on examples of good work. He may use this in the final section of the session. Experience suggests he should only intervene in the small group activities when this is essential.)

LISTENING

Failure to listen is a cause of tension between teacher and pupils. Some pupils seem to be pursued by the cry, 'Why on earth don't you listen?' throughout their school career. Yet we offer them no systematic training in what is a key skill for success. One suspects

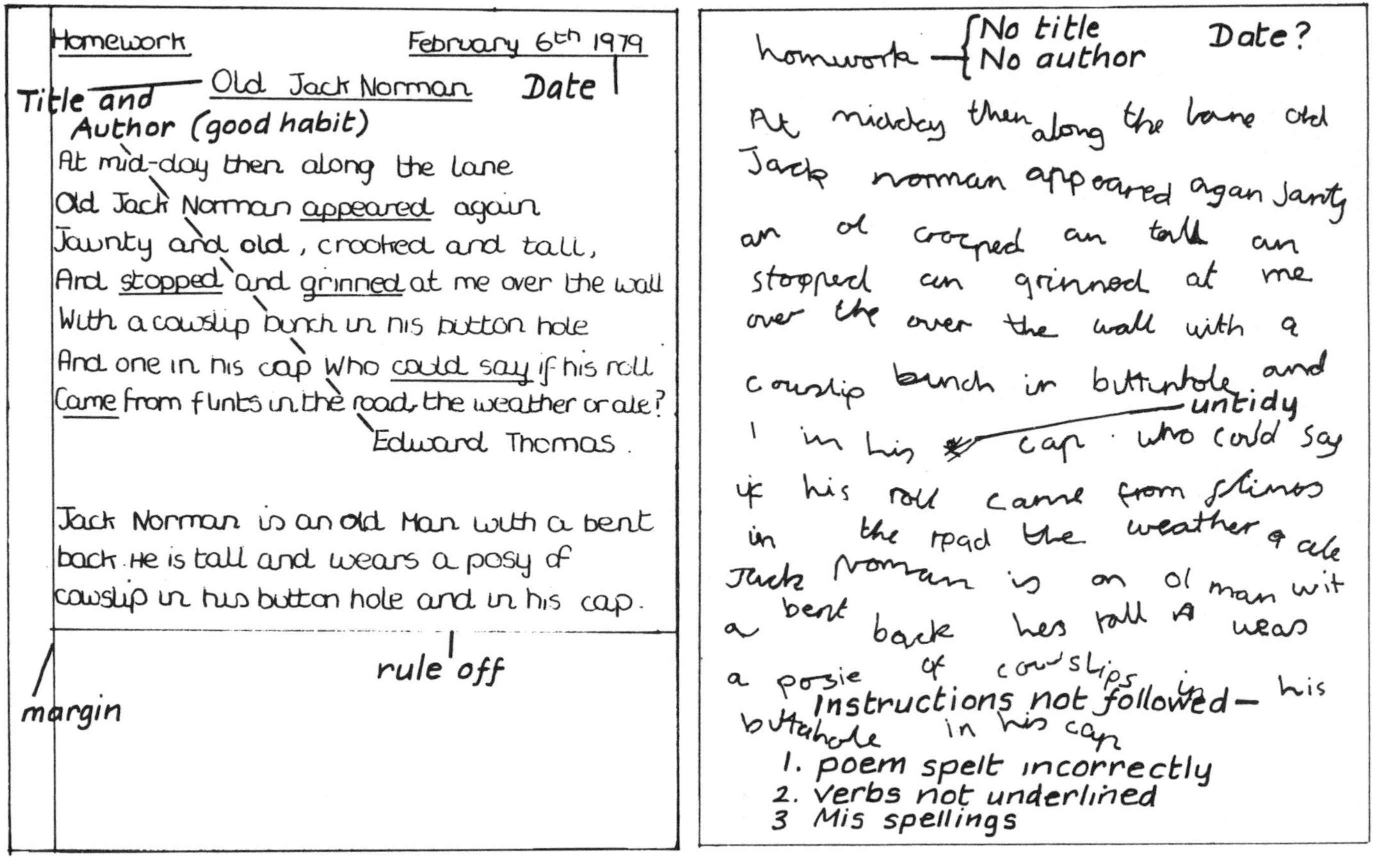

Figure 6 Homework: copy out the poem as it is written in your book, and write a few sentences about what you think the poet is saying. Underline all the verbs.

that even the educated regard such skills as listening not as acquired adroitness, but as attributes or personality qualities which either are or are not possessed.

A general package of activities inducing listening skills is provided below, preceded by an introductory activity. Listening skills are particularly important in the first two years of the secondary school because they provide the foundation for
– following instructions competently;
– correct orientation to the task;
– ensuring maximum recall of what is heard;
– detection of key ideas;
– aiding the development of new ideas and inferential thinking.
The reader will see the need to develop these skills, all based on listening, if academic success is to be achieved. Even at A-Level pupils fail to observe the rubrics, or in earlier years find themselves in difficulty when undertaking a project or holiday task because they misunderstand its nature and therefore tackle it inappropriately. The sorry failure that ensues can often be traced back to a failure in listening. Indeed, under-functioning is sometimes associated with a well-established habit of not listening or faulty listening. We claim that broadcasts and classroom instruction should generate new ideas, but a prerequisite for this is the ability to recall what they have heard and then to discriminate between the salient and the peripheral.

Activity 8
Objectives: (a) To direct pupils' attention to the importance of listening; (b) To encourage them to take the standpoint of the teacher.
A brief tape recording of two to three minutes' duration is made, in which a teacher is heard giving books back to pupils after marking. One pupil receives praise for carrying out a task competently. Another is commended for effort, although the teacher points out he has not listened to instructions and therefore has not got a good mark. Yet another is reprimanded because he has not listened to the key points in the lesson – it being made clear that this is the usual state of affairs.

This activity recognizes that pupils are often unable to see things from the perspective of the teacher. Passive acceptance of this fact merely perpetuates the *status quo*; therefore the activity pushes pupils into seeing the teacher's point of view.

First, they are asked to imagine they are the teacher and then discuss in small groups the reasons for his/her remarks. What motives does the teacher have? Then they are asked to discuss what advice they would give to pupils if they were the teacher, and to state as clearly and precisely as possible what he should do.

After five to eight minutes' small group discussion, the tutor intervenes and begins to collect ideas on the blackboard. The small groups then select and discuss those which they think will be of use to them during the next week. The teacher, who has been moving from group to group during the discussion, highlights two or three ideas he has heard being discussed by groups, stressing their application and making any appropriate suggestions.

Activity 9

Objectives: (a) To draw attention to a fairly common way of coping with the results of inattention; (b) To help pupils see that this is an immature way of responding.

An amusing cartoon is prepared as a transparency or as a duplicated handout. A car is just about to disappear under the surface of a river. The driver is saying to the passenger, 'I thought you said the red lines were rivers and the blue lines were roads!' Small groups then discuss occasions on which they have recently used the phrase, 'I thought you/he/she said . . .' in the context of homework or some other school activity. If their use of it had been associated with failure or trouble how would they prevent it from happening again? To consolidate the previous activity they are also asked how they would respond to the remark if they were the teacher.

The form tutor who, as usual, has been listening to the small group discussions, then gathers together the major reasons for the use of the statement, structuring the discussion by indicating ways in which resort to this defensive remark can be made superfluous. Due attention should be given to the reinforcement of helpful ideas produced in small group discussions.

Activity 10

Objective: To provide controlled experience of listening and checking on recall.

This is a first step in training pupils to listen. The form is divided into pairs. One partner talks about something in which he is interested and his friend listens attentively. After five to seven minutes, the form tutor stops the speakers, and the listener now has to repeat as fully as possible what the speaker said. The latter corrects errors made by the listener and at the end reminds him of any points he has omitted.

Activity 11
Objectives: (a) To provide practice in recall; (b) To draw attention to the importance of recalling items in the correct sequence.
A tape is prepared in which pupils listen to a list of five to seven simple instructions such as:

'Write – the number 946;
　　　 – the word 'read' backwards;
　　　 – the sum of 7 and 15;
　　　 – the second and fourth letters of 'British'.

They then attempt to carry out these instructions, and the tape is played again. They see how many things they have remembered, and also if they have put them in the correct order. One point is gained for each item correctly recalled, and another point is awarded if it appears in the correct position. This activity is more difficult than it appears. Some pupils will have difficulty in bearing two variables in mind simultaneously, therefore in early practices it may be helpful to introduce each item by saying, 'One: Take 14 from 28. Two: make two words out of the word *mention*.' The activity can be increased in difficulty by increasing the number of items. Obviously, the list will have to be completely different each time, otherwise pupils would be learning the earlier items off by heart and their listening and recall skills would not be extended.

This activity will be unprofitable and merely entertain unless the form tutor brings out the need to develop listening skills and links recall with testing oneself in homework assignments.

Activity 12
Objective: To show the importance of recall over a period of time.
Towards the end of a tutorial period some instructions are given for the next day. Although research is unclear whether primacy or recency is more important in aiding recall, it seems that final instructions are more likely to be remembered. Pupils are told they cannot write them down, but they should try and hold them in mind. After the teacher has issued the instructions the pupils discuss in small groups how they can remember them without committing them to writing. The next day they follow

the instructions as best they can. Within small groups, after initial individual trials, they then help one another.

The teacher then holds a general discussion on the importance of remembering instructions and encourages pupils to contribute ideas.

(It is possible that some pupils may suggest the idea of a mnemonic – if this happens the tutor should accept it and praise the individuals who thought of it. At this stage, however, it is better if the tutor himself does not introduce this aid.)

Activity 13
Objectives: (a) To train in listening and recall; (b) To link this with classroom and academic work in a direct way.
Although this is called one activity, like Activity 11 it will be spread over a number of form periods. Tapes are prepared containing either interesting material relevant to the interests of the age group or a story with strong dramatic content. At first, in this series of exercises, the equivalent of 'natural breaks' in television will occur. Pupils listen attentively to the tape and at the break write down the key points. The teacher provides *immediate feedback* by producing a list of key points, and pupils check their recall. All this is done quickly and competently, so the lists must be prepared in advance. To write the list on the blackboard would waste time.

As pupils gain experience and their ability develops they should have the number of breaks reduced. The tutor must adjust this to suit the class, and the graduation should never be unduly severe. Later in these exercises, pupils write down the key points or main ideas as they listen. Content of the tapes should be similar to that experienced in class. Again, the later stages of this activity prepare pupils for later co-operative work in raising the level of aspiration. They work in pairs, checking each other's work at the end of the exercise.

Final discussion by the tutor would draw attention to the need to look for signposts, e.g., first, second and third; the importance of paying especial attention to the first sentence which follows a pause; and learning to register what follows after such phrases as 'most important'.

Activity 14
Objectives: (a) To combine listening with the development of inferen-

tial thinking; (b) To begin to inculcate the habit of raising questions about what is read.

In this activity listening is combined with the stimulation of inferences. Short recordings of narratives are made and pupils have their attention drawn to certain points by preliminary remarks such as:

> 'As you listen try to decide what would have happened if such and such had not occurred';
>
> 'Detect the point in the story at which . . .';
>
> 'During the tape try to decide what would have occurred if such and such had happened.'

In other tapes we encourage pupils to make up questions to ask a partner. We provide them with examples which stress:

> – application of knowledge;
>
> – the making of inferences based on the content of the tape;
>
> – questions which imply a counter-argument.

This type of activity is essential because learning to raise questions about what one listens to is crucial if learning is not to be an inert process. Writers such as Robinson (1970) and Rowntree (1970) stress this when writing for students taking further and higher courses of education. Yet the form tutor can help pupils develop this vital skill in the first and second years. The activities must always be backed by the form tutor's exposition of the need to take a questioning approach to what one learns.

READING SKILLS

The approach to reading presented here is a limited one; there is no intention of trying to achieve in pastoral periods what should be accomplished by the skilled teacher of English. Here we are not concerned with speed reading as such, but with helping pupils take a more active approach to reading. They should, in guidance for success programmes, be encouraged to look for the 'heart of the problem or topic' in order to begin asking themselves questions which allow them to assess the implications of the text and examine its validity.

Reading involves both the visual and auditory – a fact which becomes evident when we reach a difficult passage. We then tend to slow down, finding that we are pronouncing each word to savour the significance and as an aid to understanding the passage fully. Speed in reading, by itself, may therefore be less important than is sometimes suggested. Many sixth form pupils do complain they 'can't get their reading done on time', but in study skills programmes they tend to be those who cannot organize themselves and therefore do not make time available. Even more frequently, I find they have to read passages two or three times before they have extracted the general meaning. Inert approaches, coupled with a feeling that learning is something 'done to them', contribute more to their difficulties than a lack of speed. Indeed, speed without the skills generating meaning is a recipe for unproductive reading.

Our concern within the guidance setting is to orientate pupils towards tasks involving reading in a way which facilitates comprehension and reinforces a positive picture of themselves as learners. Somewhat amusingly, we can see ourselves as helping pupils move towards the position of the Christ Church man, who, as Dean Chadwick claimed (Observer, 3rd September 1978) does not read a book. He *uses* it!

The SQ3R method has been developed by Robinson (1970) over a considerable period. Many readers will recognize that it is also incorporated into certain reading materials. Certainly it is a method which seems to yield results and with which pupils should be acquainted. The SQ3R approach can be represented as follows:

```
                SURVEY
            ↗          ↘
  SQ3R                   QUESTION → READ → RECALL → REVIEW
            ↘          ↗
             SCAN
```

Embodied in it is the old principle of *gestalt* psychology which stresses the need to get a grasp of the nature of the whole before attempting to master specific parts of that whole. The first step of survey and scan means that the pupil learns to look purposefully through what has to be read, building up a framework within which he can assimilate the details. All too often, even towards the final years of school, pupils read blindly without any sense of direction. Extraction of meaning is then a haphazard process, strengthening the tendency to fail to distinguish between the central and the marginal. We should encourage pupils to:

a   Note headings to get an idea of the main content and structure. The headings can be turned into questions, e.g. 'Climate and main crops' becomes, 'What crops will or will not grow in this climate? (This is another simple but neglected skill.)

b Look at the first or last paragraphs to get an idea of the content.

c Skim through the passage rapidly.

The next step is crucial. Once the pupil has gained an idea of the nature of the content we should *train* him to begin to ask questions about what he is going to read:

a What do I know about this topic already?

b What are the main themes or ideas which come up in the headings?

c What do I think I shall learn?

Obviously, this alerts pupils to the main ·ideas they will encounter, but more important is the fact that it gives them a sense of purpose, and also relates what they already know to what is to be learned. Also, the word *train* does imply practice. Although we do not impose methods on pupils we must give them sufficient practice to acquire skill before they decide to use it or not.

Attention has to be given to the idea of looking at sub-headings and turning them into questions. The pupil then reads actively to answer those questions. Progress then requires the pupil to make the recall and review parts of the task productive. Note-taking during reading can either be a distraction or may consist merely of copying out portions of the text which have not been assimilated. If this seems too extreme a statement, consultation with a university teacher will produce evidence of students who apparently believe that learning is largely a matter of indiscriminate regurgitation. Guidance on how to read early in the secondary school can help to eliminate this distressing state of affairs.

Activity 15

Objectives: (a) To induce an active search for key ideas while the individual is reading; (b) To link the auditory and visual.

This activity cannot be conducted in the form period, but pupils can be told about it and then try it at home. Most pupils possess or have access to a tape recorder, although we often ignore this in our homework assignments. We ask pupils to put key ideas and phrases on tape as they read. At the end, they test themselves by writing down the key points, finally checking them against their recorded list.

Pupils can prepare for this by writing down the key words on one half of a folded piece of paper. They then test themselves by writing down the key points they can remember on the other

Family Tree Diagram.

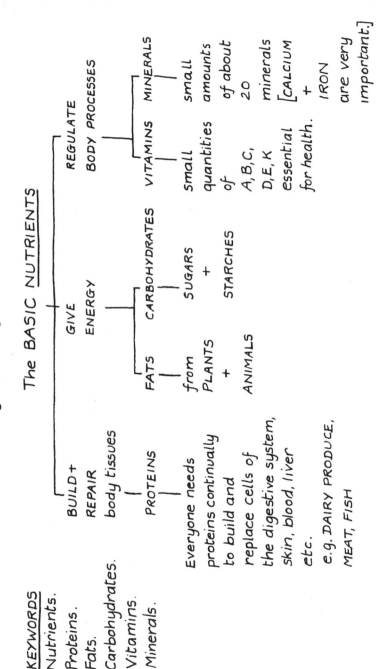

Figure 7 Family tree diagram.

part. Finally, they reveal their original list and check against it. We should train them to note what they forget, asking themselves why. Omissions can be significant and pupils need to think about them.

Activity 16
Objectives: (a) To introduce the idea of using diagrams as a means of recall; (b) To inculcate further the habit of testing oneself after reading.
This is introduced by the teacher giving the group an example of a 'family tree' diagram in which the main topic is divided into its components (see example opposite). Pupils fold a piece of paper in half. On the left hand portion the pupil writes down key words, etc. He then tests himself by building on the right hand side a family tree diagram which contains the gist of what he has learned. He then checks against his original list.

At this point reading skills very obviously merge with those of homework, because more emphasis is being placed in the reading exercises on the recall and test elements. As we have seen, pupils tend to see homework as a ritual performance rather than one which actively involves them. Self-testing as an integral part of homework has been insufficiently stressed. There is, however, no reason why this should be a solemn or unduly earnest business. This leads us to the next activity – the spider diagram.

Activity 17
Objectives: (a) To develop the skill of constructing and using the spider diagram; (b) To show its uses in recall and planning.
This diagram allows pupils to test themselves in an amusing way (Fig 8). It has the advantage of enabling pupils to process what they have learned in a way which gives it a structure partially emanating from the pupil. Consequently the likelihood of longer-term recall is increased, although the emphasis should be on its function as a convenient way of organizing what has been learned and as a test of immediate recall.

Many pupils learn better visually than through unsupported auditory recall, and they will therefore enjoy this method. For others, whose visual capacities are not so strong, the spider diagram is still a palatable way of testing and organizing information because it does not invoke spatial relationships as an integral part of processing. If, however, pupils do not respond

SPIDER DIAGRAM

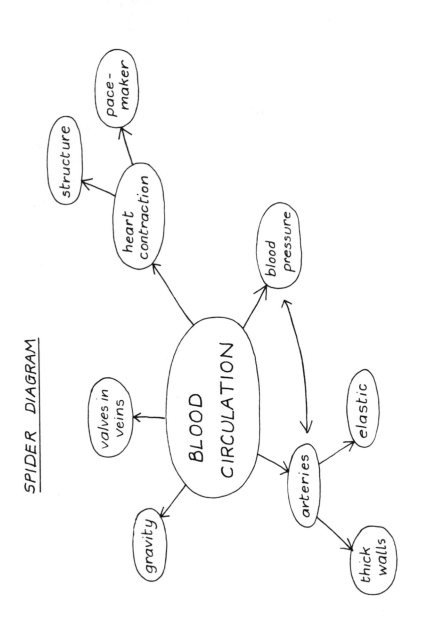

Figure 8   Spider diagram.

after due trial to a particular device, we should not compel them to use it.

First year pupils respond well to the amusing idea that we are going to look at our spider from above, and although we are probably not going to give it eight legs we will do our best to provide as many as we can. We must see they are strong enough and we must help it be as stable as possible. The steps are:

a Pupils write in the topic on which they are going to test themselves in the oval which forms the body of the spider.

b They then begin to think of the main points which they should remember and write them in as the legs. They number them in the order in which they appeared in the text or which they think is appropriate.

c The next step is to find ways of strengthening each leg by writing in key words or phrases which can act as triggers to memory.

The tutor and the pupils can adapt this idea in various ways once the basic idea has been understood. It encourages the structure and order in which many pupils may be lacking because each main point or 'leg' is the equivalent of the topic sentence opening up a paragraph. Elaboration of this topic is provided by the 'feet' which in fact are the content of the paragraph.

Activity 18
Objectives: (a) To provide experience of diagrams which emphasize the relationships between facts; (b) To build a foundation for the use of flow diagrams in later schoolwork.
The 'family tree' diagram already illustrated highlights connections and descent – hence its name. Pupils quickly see the way in which links are brought out, and appreciate the derivations implicit in the idea of descent.

Such diagrams can be used to summarize lessons and are not confined to testing how well one has understood or can recall what has been read.

The concentration on relationships in this last diagram raises certain issues. First, the combination of differing rates of intellectual and social development in conjunction with varied preferences for the visual, kinaesthetic and auditory modes of learning means that some pupils will not be ready to use diagrams unless they are given support. For some they will be an intimidating mystery and for others they may be unduly constraining. Our task of extending the skills of learning is one

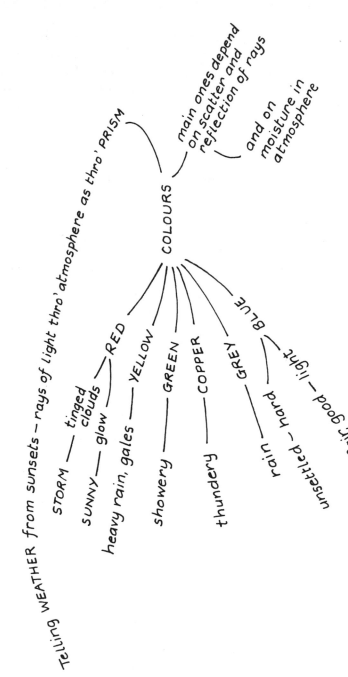

Figure 9 Taking a line for a walk.

where we must be aware of the need to adapt to the individual. Initial experimentation is a prerequisite for some pupils. Fortunately, a simple technique used in primary art helps – 'take a line for a walk' (Fig 9). In this, the pupil moves a brush charged with paint across the paper according to his momentary impulse. A pattern is then built around this line. Similarly, the pupil writes a key word or phrase, adds another to it, seeing 'where it goes' as one first year boy expressed it. Associations are likely to emerge in a spontaneous way, and it is often surprising how much is recalled – often refuting one's beliefs about a pupil!

Pupils should always have the opportunity to develop their own style. Great enthusiasm is engendered by a session in which pupils are invited to explain their way of using diagrams to the rest of the class. Such activities are a test of what is being achieved, and whether a healthy climate of experiment is developing. Tutors should be clear that such an activity tells themselves at least as much about their approach as it does about the pupils.

While it would be false to talk about what is an essential tool as 'mere memory', the tutor will see that it is a means to an·end rather than an end in itself. The pupil will have to acquire the skill of inference, the ability to go beyond the framework of immediate knowledge to apply it and see its significance in other contexts. Sixth form work demands that pupils question assumptions, examine the apparently self-evident critically, appraise positions and evaluate evidence, whether or not they are studying the sciences. Scientific thinking has never been the prerogative of the scientist alone.

Readers may over-estimate the difficulty of fostering inferential thought as an aspect of study skills. Apprehensions will be dispelled by the fact that this writer more than twenty years ago found it possible to induce this skill in 8–10 year olds receiving remedial education. Amongst other things, this was achieved through simple work cards which asked them such questions as:

- Did they think the people lived happily ever after – why? What evidence did they use?
- What do they think would have happened to them in ten years' time?
- What would have been the consequences if certain things had happened?

In every card the *why?* was stressed, bringing speculation and evidence together. Surely what is possible with 8 year olds can be achieved with 11–13 year olds if planned guidance is available?

Simple activities such as those below offer a groundwork for developing this style of thought, provided that the tutor consistently reinforces the purposes of the activity in his section of the guidance period.

Activity 19
Objectives: (a) To help pupils discover the implications of statements; (b) To encourage the sharing of speculations and the combining of inferences into a coherent story.
This activity uses simple statements which form the stimulus for a story. Pupils have to examine the implications of the statement if they are to be successful. Small groups of 3–4 pupils are allowed 10–15 minutes for the planning. One example of a 'starter' sentence is:
They came to the village at last. All was still and quiet.
This would call into play questions about *who* came. Why had they come? What is the significance of *at last*? Why was it still and quiet? Was this quiet peaceful or sinister?

Other examples of the type of sentence used to evoke inferential thinking are:
He stood stock still! Many thoughts were racing through his mind.
or:
Despite all her good intentions she'd done it again.
Readers can refer to Hamblin's (1974) description of life space plays.

The skill of the tutor is crucial in helping pupils detect and use this approach. He should demonstrate the importance of examining such statements carefully and assessing their possible meaning. Later this can be related to tests and examinations.

Activity 20
Objectives: (a) To encourage pupils to inspect contradictory data and examine the way to resolve the problems presented; (b) To create awareness of the way in which they attribute characteristics to others through simple data.
The class is presented with a list of articles found in a suitcase abandoned at the roadside. Pupils work in small groups to construct a personality picture of the kind of person who owned the suitcase. Mention can also be made of the type, condition and

quality of the case. With a little thought, articles can be included in the list which suggest contradictory or difficult-to-relate characteristics, e.g. boxing gloves (men's size, obviously used) and a spray for asthma. Groups construct character sketches, and after this they are asked to examine the inferences they have drawn. At first, the tutor structures this by raising specific questions about the contradictory items.

The tutor's contribution is vital because he must create awareness of the process of attribution, the likelihood of errors, and the possibility that alternative explanations exist and different inferences could be drawn from the same data.

Contrasting shopping baskets, or the different contents of two handbags, may provide a follow-up. In both cases pupils are asked to draw conclusions about the owners.

Activity 21
Objectives: (a) To help pupils question the validity of judgements; (b) To allow them to see the nature of the evidence which triggers off assumptions about people.
The form is presented with the picture of a room. Their task is to decide what kind of people use this room. The small groups are asked to include discussion about:
   a the kinds of friends the occupants have;
   b the kind of life they lead;
   c what people think of them.

This may appear vague and yet pupils come to conclusions on the basis of minimal cues or evidence. In the class discussion led by the tutor the pupils should be helped to explore what they focus on in making judgements, and hopefully to question the validity of the inferences which underlie their assessments. Again, the tutor must bring issues out into the open. Passivity could reinforce prejudiced or inadequate judgements and strengthen fallacious inferential processes. Reliance upon providing the activity alone could be counter-productive.

Activity 22
Objectives: (a) To help pupils become aware of some of their latent assumptions about progress in school; (b) To relate inferential thinking to learning.
This activity relates the drawing of inferences to pupils' beliefs about progress in school. The tutor presents the following dia-

gram on a transparency to the class:

YEAR	1	2	3	4	5
AVERAGE POSITION FOR YEAR IN CLASS	3	1	5	26	24

Pupils are told that this table is a record of a pupil's position in school during the first five years of his secondary education. They are asked to discuss in small groups what they think happened to him. Much emerges about their beliefs about progress, success and the significance of position in class. Very good discussions can follow on the difficulties posed by promotion, and feelings about loss of friends which can be feared as a consequence of change of class. This activity is more suitable for the second year than the first year, although it can be used if the tutor points out that people do not necessarily stay with the same form. Provided the tutor plays his part in the final discussion by reinforcing pupils' desire for success, this activity can be a valuable foundation for later work on achievement motivation.

Activity 23
Objectives: (a) To draw attention to the way in which minimal cues trigger off judgements; (b) To learn the need to check evidence on which we base conclusions.
A 3–4 minute tape recording is played in which two people with contrasting voices are heard speaking about an interesting, although not controversial, topic. Variation in accents and also a different quality of tone of voice are the relevant differences. For the latter, one might have somebody with a rasping, loud voice contrasted with a speaker who is hesitant and who tends to have high-pitched speech. Flatness, resonance or warmth are other relevant qualities. Pupils are instructed to try to gain an impression of the character and personality of each speaker as they listen. At the end, they build up personality pictures using key words or phrases.

In small groups they explain to each other what judgements they came to, and on what evidence they were based. After this the tutor intervenes, asking pupils to suggest what characteristics influenced them. Four to six are then selected and written on the board. Pupils will often be imprecise: 'How he talked – it was posh!' Friendly questioning usually produces clarification. Finally the discussion focuses on the validity or fallibility of such cues as triggers for judgement.

Activity 24
Objective: To encourage pupils to anticipate and assess possibilities.
The class are asked to work in pairs. The tutor asks them to imagine that they have been telephoning a friend and have been cut off. What do they do? Their task is that of working out all the possibilities, e.g. does A wait for B to ring back, but is B doing the same? If they ring to find it engaged what does this mean? Do they both dial immediately?

The tutor helps the class build up the possibilities on the blackboard. He then relates this way of thinking to relevant homework and learning situations.

Activity 25
Objective: To help pupils achieve greater flexibility in associating objects together.
Pupils are given three objects which have no obvious link and are asked to blend them into a story. They must have a central position in the plot and not be confined to a marginal position. Examples are:

   a a stick of liquorice; a red blanket; a saw.
   b a used birthday card; a wheelbarrow; a street lamp.

Association rather than inference is being stressed here. Yet this exercise has proved very productive in getting pupils to think more in planning essays and stories, provided the tutor highlights the processes involved, making pupils aware of them and their power to think.

A note on the preceding activities

Many of the most successful activities stimulating inferential thought in this age group are those built around the need to appreciate the nature of relationships between people and understand the nature of processes of judgement and person perception. Pupils have to cope with a sudden expansion in the range and type of their social relationships when they enter the secondary school. Growing self-awareness produces the realization in many that their former simplistic criteria for assessing the motives of others are becoming inadequate. Killing two birds with one stone is a chancy operation, yet it seems to be the fact that the form tutor has a pay-off for these activities which is not confined to the intellectual field. The rewards are increased when the tutor makes the links explicit to the pupils.

SPECIAL ASPECTS OF GUIDANCE IN THE SECOND YEAR

Experienced teachers are aware that in the second year some pupils develop negative attitudes to school, work, self and other people, that are not translated into behaviour until later in the secondary school. This writer and his students recently undertook a questionnaire type survey of approximately 850 pupils in thirteen comprehensive schools as a prelude to devising a general framework of guidance for the second year.

Study skills cannot be separated from other aspects of development. Puberty is associated with the acquisition of a sense of identity, while the boundaries between what is self and what is alien are of special significance. In our study, which was supplemented by discussion with the classes involved, we found that this group were easily exasperated and susceptible to aggravation from other pupils. They felt that they were in danger of losing control, while tensions within the family seemed to be developing. Informal discussions suggested that this proneness to irritability was likely to be the product of the onset of puberty and/or the conflict between the need for dependence and the desire for autonomy. It was interesting that many of them made reference to the fact that younger brothers and sisters were 'pests' who impinged on their privacy and invaded their territory.

Next, there seemed to be growing uncertainty in the fields of self-confidence and social confidence. These seemed to focus very sharply on the following.

1 Fears and hesitancies about speaking out in a crowd or class, sometimes coupled with the fear of being wrong or alarm at sounding 'funny'.
2 Difficulties about saying what they really feel or think, resulting in gross over-reaction or dissembling.

It is possible that these factors push the second year pupil into over-reliance on the peer group and stultify his capacity for spontaneity in learning. The worry the children expressed about the impression they create and their sensitivity to what others think of them need to be taken into account in the programme of guidance for achievement. Incidentally, the study also showed that presentation of work seemed to be a problem for a large proportion of the sample. Difficulties were also reported with note-taking, structuring essays and answers to questions and revision skills.

The discussions suggested that the guidance programme should supplement the study skills element by dealing with the factors set out below. Pupils were clear that they were sources of difficulty which influenced their capacity to absorb information in the classroom and respond positively to the teacher.

1 Learning to cope with frustration without putting themselves into positions from which it is difficult to withdraw or which bring costly consequences.

2 Dealing with loss of face, especially when a friend or attractive group is the source of threat.

3 Managing pressures from the peer group or friends to indulge in behaviour which they find distasteful or guilt-producing. It seemed that those pupils surveyed found the element of moral blackmail based on friendship particularly difficult to cope with.

4 Understanding the standpoint of parents and recognizing the concern behind prohibitions. Partially expressed hostility against parents can be brought into school. The pupil from the good home can sometimes punish his parents by developing a cavalier attitude to achievement.

5 Coping with the pressure towards conformity to the norms of a class group. This includes the element of safety involved in the fear of being labelled a 'ponce'.

6 The demands of friendship which are restrictive, perhaps best expressed in the questions, 'Do I have to be everything that my friends expect me to be?' and 'What are the limits to friendship?'

It is in the second year that the peer group begins to exercise on the individual its coercive influence, which he often appears unable to resist because of developmental factors. Without dealing with these forces, study skills are unlikely to be used constructively by those to whom they are offered.

CAN WE IMPROVE THE CONTRIBUTION OF TESTS AND EXAMINATIONS TO ACHIEVEMENT?

Assessment, evaluation and anxiety are closely associated: indeed, we sometimes view them as inseparable. Birney *et al.* (1969) show that anxiety and the need for achievement based on immature factors combine in *fear of failure*. The result is learning lacking the dynamism of active striving for success. Instead it is impelled by fear of the consequences of failing to meet the real or imagined expectations of others. This is very close to the position of Sarason *et al.* (1958), who stress the importance of anticipated disapproval by parents, teachers and peers in the production of text anxiety. More directly, Banks and Finlayson (1973) have demonstrated that it is not paternal interest *per se* that is of importance in underfunctioning, but how the father manifests his concern. It is not solely the objective reactions of the parent which are central, however, for the perceptions of the significance of parental behaviour differ from child to child. This is just as true of tests and examinations as it is of parents, and highlights the need for a programme of guidance for success to examine the question of anxiety in relation to them and (where the association is unproductive) take steps to deal with it.

The influence of anxiety on behaviour is discussed elsewhere (Hamblin, 1974; 1978). Anxiety can be seen primarily as a response to some threat: it is a signal of danger. The obvious step is then to locate the specific sources of danger. Phillips (1978), in a valuable discussion of school stress and anxiety, points out that the elements of competition and comparison found in tests are sources of stress for many pupils. This may be a situation which is a derivative or extension of the less easily detected unease about answering questions in class. The guidance programme should therefore include a discussion of pupils' feelings about being asked questions, the sense of losing face, and the fact, as Gaudry and Spielberger (1971) suggest, that the pupil who is anxious about tests can end up in an examination paying more attention to his feelings of anxiety than to the task itself. A little thought and observation will show that this applies even more to the revision and preparation stages, for it is at this stage most pupils experience anxiety. Hence the very anxious pupil can doom himself to failure unless helped.

The simple diagram set out below (Fig. 10) indicates the main factors that the form tutor must have in mind. The pupil marked by *trait* anxiety will need more prolonged support and individual counselling. In terms of the systematic approach to guidance which underlies this book, the tutor will concentrate on the situations which provoke anxiety and the behaviours which lead to underfunctioning or failure in tests and examinations.

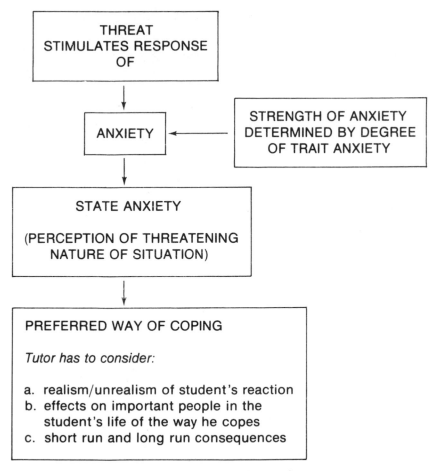

THREAT
STIMULATES RESPONSE
OF

ANXIETY

STRENGTH OF ANXIETY
DETERMINED BY DEGREE
OF TRAIT ANXIETY

STATE ANXIETY

(PERCEPTION OF THREATENING
NATURE OF SITUATION)

PREFERRED WAY OF COPING

Tutor has to consider:

a. realism/unrealism of student's reaction
b. effects on important people in the
   student's life of the way he copes
c. short run and long run consequences

Figure 10

The diagram makes it clear that we can intervene to change the individual's perceptions of a threatening situation and also that we can help cope more effectively. A fuller knowledge of situations reduces the ambiguity which seems to be a concomitant of anxiety and which may be related to its severity. Discussion of such situations as reading aloud in class can – to a surprisingly large degree – immunize the individual against adverse emotional reactions. Immunization and anticipation may be useful, but with some pupils, they will be insufficient. Hence we need to examine the pupils' current strategies for coping and teach them new ones. Pupils react to threat in varied ways: attack involving displacement of resentment on to parents or teachers; avoidance, often taking the form of procrastination; or a determined attempt to develop the necessary skills, represent just three out of a wide range of possibilities. Anxiety can lead to actions which facilitate achievement, or which progressively enfeeble the individual by reducing his attempts to cope (day-dreaming is often the product of anxiety from which the pupil has to escape) and also encourages the growth of self-derogating attitudes which restrict actions.

Phillips (1978) found that pupils felt that the teacher went too fast for them; that they worked hardest when they knew that their results would be compared with those of others; that teacher and parental expectations were intimidating; but the possibility of making an error when questioned by the teacher also seemed to be a major source of stress. This means that we have to achieve a balance between adapting to the pupil and building their capacity to cope. But even if anxiety is not a problem, it is still essential that we allow pupils to discuss examinations and the ways in which they cope. If the style of thought and problem solving is to be the subject of creative enquiry in the sixth form, then a start has to be made early in the comprehensive school which inculcates the habit of analysing problems of learning.

We have seen that the sense of being compared and assessed is strongly linked with anxiety about tests. Anxiety is not only a response to danger, but it is a case of passivity and task avoidance. Our guidance programme should help pupils to:

a understand the need for evaluation;
b learn to deal with tests competently through planned study;
c examine the mechanisms they use when faced with a test or examination, which may include:
  – attack as a response to feeling anxious;
  – avoidance, including putting off working and other forms of procrastination;
  – appealing for sympathy;
  – blaming others.

The need to discuss does not mean that we will give easy reassurance or collude with pupils to help them avoid self-criticism. It does mean that we train pupils to take responsibility for their own fate and to strive actively to improve their methods of working.

Activity 26
Objectives: (a) To help pupils assess their difficulties; (b) To provide a simple framework for discussing them.
A checklist is a useful structuring device for a discussion and subsequent activities. The one given below has proved to be useful.

HOMEWORK, TESTS AND ME

What to do:
Read each statement carefully. Then if you think it is like you, put a tick in the LIKE ME box. If it is not you, put a tick in the NOT LIKE ME box.

	LIKE ME	NOT LIKE ME
1 I can't seem to get my homework done on time.	☐	☐
2 I worry a lot the night before a test.	☐	☐
3 I seem to lose marks because my work is untidy.	☐	☐
4 I lose marks in tests because I always seem to forget what I know.	☐	☐
5 I sometimes think I am the only one in the class who finds the tests hard.	☐	☐
6 I always seem to do the wrong thing (e.g. in the last test we were told to write a paragraph, but I wrote a whole essay).	☐	☐
7 I think people will laugh at me if I read aloud in class.	☐	☐
8 I don't like to tell the teacher when I can't do my work.	☐	☐
9 I always seem to make a lot of careless mistakes.	☐	☐
10 I worry if I think I am going to have to answer a question in class.	☐	☐
11 When I am playing I sometimes find myself wondering if I have done my homework right.	☐	☐
12 I often spend a whole evening trying to do my maths.	☐	☐
13 I spend a lot of time getting ready for a test, but it doesn't seem to help much.	☐	☐
14 I'm scared to ask my parents to help me in case people say I'm cheating.	☐	☐

NOW:
1 Choose FOUR of the items you have ticked as LIKE YOU. Write them in order of difficulty in the box below, beginning with the one you think will be easiest to put right.

2 Then discuss what you could do to put the first one right with a friend.

3 Write out the steps you will take in the lower half of the box.

```
THE THINGS I FIND DIFFICULT:

1 (Easiest)   _____
2             _____
3             _____
4 (Hardest)   _____
              _____
```

```
WHAT I CAN DO TO PUT THE EASIEST ONE RIGHT:




```

The teacher will include a general discussion in which he suggests that pupils should think very carefully and write down precisely what they will do. Vague statements such as 'Work harder', 'Improve my spelling' or 'Stop worrying' are shown to be of little use. Instead, 'Test myself after I finish my homework each evening', 'Find four words every day that I seem to keep getting wrong and learn them' or 'Keep a homework diary in which I write down instructions' are shown to be more profitable.

Activity 27
Objective: To help pupils develop ways of coping with a source of learning difficulty
The next step consists of a tutor preparing a tape of about 3–5 minutes' duration. This centres on just *one* source of difficulty that the tutor has noted as being fairly common as a result of the previous activity. The tape presents as a narrative the attempts of someone who decided to tackle the situation. For example, if the problem was that of spending time preparing for tests, but still getting poor results, it could be suggested that he:

a stopped complaining about the unfairness of life and asked himself why he wasn't getting results;

b decided to make a revision timetable which was realistic and methodical;

  c started to test himself as he learned each evening using 'spider' or 'family tree' diagrams and also his tape recorder;

  d built up summary cards, which contained the main points of topics, as a basis for periodic tests.

Before listening, pupils are told they are going to be asked to think about what the boy is doing, evaluate it and make further suggestions. After hearing the recording, they are asked to discuss in small groups:

  a which of his ideas would work for them;

  b what they would add to his plans.

A form discussion then follows in which the tutor builds up a plan for dealing with this difficulty from the ideas offered by the class. This is done on the blackboard.

This activity is crucial because it gives pupils the opportunity to think about difficulties in a way which suggests the steps which can be taken to solve them. Like a number of the other activities, it can be repeated on a number of occasions with different content and slight variations of presentation. This can be linked with the following:

Activity 28
Objectives: (a) To introduce the idea of peer support; (b) To build on the idea of a hierarchy of difficulties by referring pupils back to the schedule.

Pupils are asked to consider the second difficulty they isolated in the checklist 'Homework, Tests and Me' (p. 61), and discuss what action they could take with a friend. After the initial discussion, they are asked to write this down in the form of a story about themselves. They are encouraged to be concrete and specific. The tutor then states that friends can work together to help one another achieve the targets. They then work out the supports they will offer to each other during the coming week.

The tutor ends by suggesting other ways of using the mutual support:

  a they might consider doing their homework and revision together;

  b they spend a few minutes each day discussing their targets and what they can do to improve the chances of achieving them.

This can be the first of a series of planning sessions where pupils begin to look at the possibility of modifying their learning behaviour. Evaluation and reinforcement of the steps taken during the week following the session is essential if anything real is to happen.

Activity 29
Objective: To help pupils appreciate the need to plan.
Simple cartoons are prepared showing a sequence of responses to the impending test or terminal examination (Figs 11, 12). These will stress:

'The test is three weeks away, I'd better do something about it.'

'Two weeks to go – I must get started tomorrow!'

'A week today, perhaps the best thing is to prepare the night before.'

'What a fool I was! I put off revising and got what I asked for – failure!'

This opens up a discussion of the tendency in us all to put off working. This may be the point at which the tutor brings out the difference between those who believe that success is the product of planning and intelligent methods of study and, those who hope it will 'turn out alright in the end' and who rely on the concept of luck. Pupils are then shown amusing cartoons of 'Mr. Let's see how things turn out' and 'Mr. Let me plan for my future'. They are then asked to write down what they think will have been achieved

– by the time they leave school;

– after ten years in work;

– by the age of 40.

This activity is very important. Sumner and Warburton (1972) found that pupils allergic to school expected the teachers to make them work. There seems to be a reliance in many pupils upon external pressures and surveillance. If this reactive approach to learning is to be replaced by a more productive one, then it seems sensible to begin to modify these attitudes as soon as possible. It is now commonplace to hear the statement that many pupils of this type come from homes where the ability to defer gratification is absent. More to the point may be the fact that many pupils – not necessarily from materially deprived homes – lack the skills of planning. Unless they are taught to tackle learning tasks in a way which allows them to achieve fairly immediate goals they are unlikely to reach more distant ones. Without the ability to set

Figure 11

themselves short-term targets they lack the momentum needed to reach long-term objectives. Such pupils often are unable to plan a revision timetable covering the ten days preceding terminal examinations. This is the subject of the next activity.

Activity 30
Objective: To help pupils plan a revision timetable.
The tutor begins by asking pupils to draw up a balance sheet of their strong, average and weak subjects. He then gives some details of what will be tested in the terminal examinations. Out-line timetables are distributed to the form covering the ten days

Figure 12

before the examinations. Before pupils begin to plan their revision strategies the tutor underlines the need to be realistic.
neither over-revising nor scamping their preparation. Next, one
day is discussed carefully, the object being to create awareness
of:

  a the need to be realistic: too much revision is as unhelpful
    as too little;
  b the danger of over-concentration on weak subjects;
  c the need to distribute learning by allowing oneself reason-
    able breaks between subjects;

d the need to alternate between easy and difficult subjects wherever possible;

e the desirability of self-testing during every period of revision.

Once these points have been dealt with, the class is asked to imagine it is about a fortnight from the exams and they have decided to work out a plan of action. At the end, if time permits, or in the next session they compare their plans in small groups. One group can then be asked to explain the merits of a plan they consider to be especially helpful.

(It has proved helpful to undertake this exercise about 3–4 weeks before pupils need to prepare a timetable for their first terminal examination. This anticipation is obviously unnecessary in later terms where all that is needed is the period for planning.)

Activity 31
Objective: To provide experience in planning an answer to examination questions.

Pupils listen to a ten-minute recording on some topic. As they do so, they make notes as indicated in the section on listening. They are then given an examination-type question. They do not, however, write out the answer in full, but make a diagram which shows the main points they would include and the order in which they would deal with them

Planning an answer is a skill some pupils fail to acquire early enough; perhaps some never do. The result is reliance upon blind forms of memorization leading to answers in which information has been inserted in the hope that it is relevant. Tutors may find it helpful to talk to the form about 'thinking in headlines'. He makes it clear that the headline subsumes other points. Therefore if we recall the headlines other points will fall into place in a relevant way.

Activity 32
Objective: To provide a simple aid for recall.

Rote recall is only one form of understanding, but unless pupils can recall the facts, they are going to be unable to draw valid inferences from them. So memory aids, despite their artificiality, assist the development of the sense of competence essential for active learning. Most pupils in the first and second years take to mnemonics with enthusiasm. Providing one shows that they are merely a tool to enable one to remember and not a substitute for reasoning, their use is legitimate.

The tutor takes a topic and talks about it for 5–8 minutes. He then asks the class to write down the key points they recall. Once this is done, he writes the key points on the board as a mnemonic. Pupils then select a topic they have been revising and try to make use of their own. They then share these with one another in their small groups. (The single word mnemonic is usually more difficult to develop than one which is a sentence in which the first letter of each word is also the initial letter of a key word belonging to the topic which has to be memorized.)

Pupils are then asked to use the technique during the week and be ready to demonstrate a mnemonic at the next guidance session.

Activity 33
Objective: To draw the different techniques together while also encouraging pupils to select what suits them.
The following situation is presented either as a narrative, taped conversation or on a duplicated sheet.

Bob and David had been good friends at their primary school, but just before the move to the comprehensive school Bob's father changed his job and the family moved to another part of the town. Just before the exams at the end of the first year they met again. Bob said he was worried about them because he had done badly at Christmas and Easter. David said he was lucky and started to tell Bob about the different ways he had learned of studying successfully. Bob decided to ask David to come home and when they got there the first thing David did was to write down ways of studying he had found helpful.
Write down what *you* think David might have written below:

A general discussion follows in which the tutor helps pupils see that people find certain techniques helpful while others do not. Therefore we need to select what is right for us; the responsibility is ours.

Activity 34

Objective: To provide pupils with the experience of making a simple diagnosis of learning difficulties.

An audiotape is prepared in which a pupil is talking to his form tutor who is reviewing his progress. Considerable concern is expressed in a positive way by the tutor, who draws attention to unattractively presented work, incomplete homework assignments, negative remarks on terminal reports and the possibility of demotion (only where this is applicable). The conversation reaches the point when the tutor says, 'Now we can do something about this. Let's begin by working out a plan for putting things right.' The narrative then stops and the form are asked to

a assess why the pupil is failing, arranging the factors involved in a hierarchy of importance;

b make suggestions about *what* the pupil should do and *how* he should do it.

SELF-MANAGEMENT

A number of skills which contribute to self-management are incorporated into the earlier sections of this chapter, e.g. checking, partnerwork and target setting. At first sight partnerwork appears to have little connection with self-management. In fact, it is a necessary step in releasing pupils from over-reliance on teachers. To be able to set your own targets, albeit in a limited way, and to give and accept advice from friends on achieving those targets is a step towards responsible autonomy. We can also reinforce self-management in other ways.

First, we can train pupils to be methodical. A lost notebook at O-Level or A-Level creates near panic. Yet all too often this is merely a specific instance of a general tendency. If the pupil has a place of his own in which homework is usually done, then he should be encouraged to treat it as a workshop. This means a place for notebooks, texts, pens, and so on. Containers for paper clips, rubber bands and other impedimenta are essential. Mothers may well feel bereft or relieved according to their personality once the familiar cry 'Can you find a ––––?' disappears. Yet it is important that it does not continue. It is the accumulation of little incidents of this type which makes homework a source of irritation for parent and child alike. The homework timetable should be fastened to the wall. It should contain simple notes such as 'Check my bag to see if I have set-squares and compasses for ––––.'

Perhaps it will be felt that this advice is impractical when the pupil lives in overcrowded and noisy conditions. In practice it becomes more important that routines and order are established when conditions are poor. Every good workman has his toolbox! Pupils can keep the books and materials in a special box. Cramped environments usually produce a strong sense of property and territory. Adolescents seem to like this idea, often stressing that they have chosen a stout box with a lid to prevent the marauding sibling from making off with pens. The homework timetable is often fastened inside the lid of the box.

Self-management includes the establishment of workable routine. Regularity is essential if performance is not to fluctuate unnecessarily. Television is regarded as the enemy of homework, but it has its uses. The ending of a programme as the signal for the commencement of homework has proved worthwhile when all else has failed. Every mother has used the device, 'You can do it after you have –––––', but pupils can apply this principle to themselves as a form of self-reward. A favourite programme is an excellent self-reward.

Another activity encouraging self-management is to ask the pupil to imagine he is the form tutor and write a brief report on his study habits, homework and attitudes to learning. This not only encourages him to take the teacher's standpoint, but asks him to look at himself more objectively. Neither negativism nor complacency is fostered by this if the pupil is asked to make concrete and specific recommendations for improvement.

Cartoons can contribute effectively to the development of self-management. Guidance should be interesting and have the vitality to which adolescents respond. Moralizing is taboo because it is counter-productive, but cartoons get the point home without arousing resistance. Another device used by Ahier (1978) is that of incorporating the activities into a series centred on two or more pupils. This narrative may give a sense of continuity in the first year, although I suspect older pupils would find it demeaning.

A final point. These activities may be tried, and found not so much to be wanting, as to be difficult. This is inevitable. Both tutors and pupils have to acquire the skills. Perhaps there is a deceptive simplicity about suggestions presented in the form set out above. Time, consistency and adequate practice are essential for success.

3: Years Three and Four

This is the time in the secondary school in which pupils begin to
dissociate actively from school, and in which underfunctioning
appears unless we are vigilant. There are three main headings
under which we can examine what is likely to impinge on performance in years three and four. These will enter into the discussion
and suggested activities.
  1 Personality and developmental factors;
  2 methods of consolidating existing study skills and extending
     them;
  3 the positive or negative contribution to achievement stem-
     ming from friends and peer group influences.
At first sight there may seem to be little to do in the field of
guidance for success and the extension of study skills. During
these two years many pupils will be struggling to achieve a sense
of identity and establish some measure of emotional independence
from their parents. The presence or absence of understanding of
developmental difficulties is particularly crucial in these years.
Constructive intervention at this point, when pupils are reshaping
their concepts of themselves as individuals, and acquiring a sense
of individuality, can strengthen their resolve to strive to attain a
standard of excellence. Lack of it may strengthen existing self-
doubt and negativism.
  In these two years large numbers of pupils experience an acute
desire to achieve autonomy, unfortunately expressing it in ways
which bring opposition from adults and are eventually self-
restricting. Erikson (1968) has described adolescence as a period of
moratorium or intermission within which pupils come to terms
with themselves. They identify with new heroes of the pop scene
and revise their evaluations of the adults who figure prominently
in their lives – parents and teachers.

It would be unrealistic to ignore the fact that in the third and fourth years the desire for immediate gratification is at its strongest. Planning ahead may seem especially unattractive when the main impulse is to live fully today. Time is an elastic concept, and two years appear to be infinity to the thirteen year old. Let us recognize realistically that some pupils will be trying to balance the pressures stemming from physical puberty and the associated upsurge of emotions, against the demands for rationality in choosing O-Level subjects and thinking about a career. Individual uncertainty is also accompanied by doubts about the wisdom of investing energy in acquiring academic qualifications in this age of economic uncertainty, although to exaggerate this may lead us into behaving in ways which persuade pupils they ought to be feeling this.

Let us maintain a sense of perspective. We should recognize that complications and anxieties stemming from physical and emotional development are often more important to our pupils than the content of our teaching. They need overt but unsentimental signs that we recognize their feelings. Young people do sometimes come from homes with rigid, traditionally orientated parents where the world is presented as essentially threatening in nature. They end up feeling that 'they themselves are the people their parents warned them against'. Our signals of acceptance are indispensable if they are to resolve this dilemma constructively.

In the middle years of the secondary school the unavoidable increase of demands may cause pupils to react by avoidance of work or misbehaviour. The fear of 'loss of face' with peers is aroused when they predict that teachers will ask questions in class which reveal their inadequacy, causing classmates amusement. They will then misbehave, distracting attention from their inability to their behaviour. This is particularly true of boys in the subjects traditionally seen as important for males. Teachers often respond by ejecting them as nuisances from the classroom, allowing them to escape from a noxious situation with the additional reward of enhanced status in the eyes of other pupils. We can see that it is only too easy to concentrate on the inconvenient behaviours, not seeing that they are defensive reactions to doubts about capacity to meet demands which are being compounded by the upsurge of emotions and insecurity produced by the physiological and psychological changes of early puberty. Pupils who are of marginal ability, especially in mathematics, chemistry and physics, are the victims of stress which they tend to cover by bravado. The fluctuations of effort stemming from their self-doubt earn them teacher reprimands. Yet encouragement and exhortation has little effect on pupils who compare themselves negatively with others in the class or who predict that effort will not yield results. When a pupil is taking a few subjects in the fifth year public examinations, it is imperative that he considers those choices in relation to his future working life. But this is necessary at a time when he is deeply confused about what he is and where he is going.

FOSTERING THE MOTIVE TO ACHIEVE

Underfunctioning may be the manifest form of negative attitudes towards school work and achievement. It may also be the product of specific learning disabilities or of inadequate teaching. We may also concentrate on intelligence in a way which obscures the problem. Naylor (1972) argues that to suggest that a pupil's intelligence in isolation inevitably predicts his level of performance, is to place over-achievement in the realm of the miraculous and to make under-functioning unduly problematic.

Major workers in the field of attitudes, Allport (1935), Fishbein (1967), McGuire (1969), Jones and Gerard (1967) and Secord and Backman (1964), lead one to conclude that:
  1 An attitude is a state of readiness to act or react in a particular way. Therefore it remains dormant until activated.
  2 Attitudes determine current and future behaviour in relation to the object of the attitude (e.g. a particular subject or type of learning task). This behaviour takes the form of (a) evaluation of the situation, person and event as potentially harmful or beneficial; (b) approach or avoidance.

It is worth spending a little time looking at attitudes, as we so frequently resort to them to explain behaviour. It is customary to assume (e.g. Krech *et al.*, 1962) that the major components of attitudes are:
  1 *cognitions* or the beliefs and opinions that the possessor of the attitude holds about the situation, individual or event;
  2 the *feelings* aroused by the actual or imagined presence of the attitude which lead to positive or negative evaluation of it;
  3 *action* directed towards approach or avoidance of the object, and, where appropriate, harming or supporting it.

This is neatly summarized by Fishbein (1967) who remarks that an attitude is the evaluative aspect of a belief. Achievement motivation is concerned with the assessment and possibility and desirability of success; so it is germane to our concerns. Achievement is also a product of the pupil's perceptions of the meaning of an activity. Kelly (1955) shows the different constructions placed on the same event by individuals. Meaning is not inherent in the event, instead it assumes meaning according to the perceptions of the individual. When we ask a pupil to engage in an activity which is within his competence, he can approach it eagerly, avoid it because he deems it repugnant, regard it with mild interest, or see it as irrelevant to his purposes.

Attitudes are used to explain the response to the learning situation, but they are only inferences. Although attitudes are conceptualized as variables which shape (or perhaps determine) behaviour, allowing us to predict what a person will do, there is not an exact correspondence between attitudes and behaviour. The situation always contains constraints or factors which either inhibit or facilitate the translation of an attitude into behaviour. Bearing this in mind, perhaps the best model to help us link achievement and development is that provided by Oppenheim (1966). The major features of the depth model are given below.

The depth model sees:
— personality and attitudes as intimately linked;
— the *concept of self* as at the heart of a person's attitudes;
— the way in which the pupil perceives and interprets his environment as crucial in shaping his responses to it;
— an attitude as purposeful, serving the needs of the individual.

The implications of the depth model are that:
1 The feelings and emotions are the salient features because they provide the energy leading to actions;
2 The self-picture of the pupil is a key to understanding the behaviour of the pupil;
3 While attitudes are organized, they are not necessarily logical.

Motivation and attitudes are concepts we resort to in explaining pupils' reactions to the classroom. Oppenheim emphasizes that attitudes are closely related to the pupil's perception of himself and the kind of person he aspires to be. The depth model again reinforces the point that the feelings behind the attitude provide the energy for approach or avoidance. In his early work on achievement motivation McClelland stresses (McClelland *et al.*, 1953) that motives have two functions. They energize behaviours, and are also directional in the sense that they guide their holder towards a specific goal.

The above comments suggest that it is imperative that we give attention to attitudes and feelings in a study skills programme if it is not to be a sterile 'bag of tricks'. Equally, if the programme is to lead to an effective individual style of learning, then the emphasis on attitudes and motives should come at the time when the adolescent is engaged in the process of reorganizing his sense of self. Leach (1965) goes further when she suggests that the identity crisis of adolescence, which seems to appear in the years under discussion, may present us with the last opportunity of modifying rigidity, early closure on problems and the tendency to dichotomize into good or bad, black or white. Intellectual efficiency is lowered by such tendencies. We seem to have a choice between accepting them, complaining about them, relying on exhortation and intervening constructively.

Katz (1960) examines the functions attitudes perform for their holders. In pastoral care we must look at the value climate of the school and the wider influences which operate to determine performance, as much as we look at the pupils. The diagram below focuses on three of the functions that Katz attributes to attitudes, raising questions about the broader context of learning that we have to answer if we are concerned with guidance for success. The head of year or house should explore these questions thoroughly with his team of tutors.

THE FUNCTIONS OF ATTITUDES

1 *Utilitarian*
   a They are adopted because they bring rewards and avoid punishment.
   b These attitudes are aroused, when demands are made upon the pupil.
   c Attitudes are modified if rewards are denied and punishment increased. More positively, we can increase meaningful rewards.

Questions relevant to achievement
1 What is the balance between rewards and punishment?
2 What rewards are available and meaningful for different groups within the school?

2 *Self-protective*
   a These are based on the need to protect their possessor against
     dangers to self-respect.
   b They are aroused by frustration and threat.
   c Change comes when the level of threat is low and pupils feel
     secure.

   Questions about self-protective attitudes
   1 What erodes or builds up the pupil's self-respect?
   2 How constrictive are the frustrations pupils meet?
   3 Do they spring from poor organization and arbitrary deci-
     sions?

3 *Self-expressive*
   a These maintain a favourable picture of their holder.
   b They are aroused by the tendency to compare oneself with
     others.
   c Change occurs as the pupil develops new ideas.

   Questions relevant to positive self-expression
   1 What identities are provided by the school for pupils?
   2 Does the school encourage positive self-expression?

Activity 35
*Objective: To help pupils explore the nature of success and examine
their beliefs about the successful learner.*
A duplicated questionnaire is produced which contains the following questions:
   1 In what ways would you like to be successful at school?
     Please give your reasons below.
   2 What kind of person do you think is likely to succeed in
     school and at work? List them in the boxes below:

SUCCESSFUL AT SCHOOL	SUCCESSFUL AT WORK

   3 *Now* choose one of these qualities *you* would like to pos-
     sess. Perhaps you have it already, but would like more of it.

Discuss in your small groups how you would set about developing it.

The tutor builds a blackboard diagram which shows the main qualities seen as important for success. Attention is drawn to any discrepancies between what is needed for success at school and what they see as relevant for success at work.

Activity 36
Objectives: (a) To help pupils see the existence of self-defeating strategies through the use of humour; (b) To relate this to the way they respond to frustration in real life situations.
First, the following cartoon (Fig 13) is presented, which shows the reaction to the frustration which comes from embarrassment.

After the laughter, the tutor points out to the form that we all experience frustration and the sense of being defeated. How we cope is vital. We have to learn to look at the long-term costs of what we do. He then reads the following to the class:

John is in the third year and is about to choose his O-Level subjects. He wants to be an engineer, but he is having difficulty with physics so he decides to drop the subject. He does not talk about it to anybody. Two years later he is thinking of trying for an apprenticeship, but he realizes he has to have physics. He then sees that his decision was not very sensible – so he decides to take O-Level physics in the sixth form.

What advice would you give someone like John who feels frustrated because they are not doing well in an important subject? Don't say 'Work harder.' Be more helpful than this.

The tutor ends by helping the form evaluate the reactions to frustration by looking at:

a the long-term consequences of their advice;
b the level of risk in it;
c what it says about whether the individual can change things;
d the way in which the expedient response may be comfortable at the moment but brings future punishment.

The use of humour allows us to breach defensive attitudes in a constructive way. It is a tool – a means and not an end in itself. We therefore follow it up immediately by an activity which extends the point made.

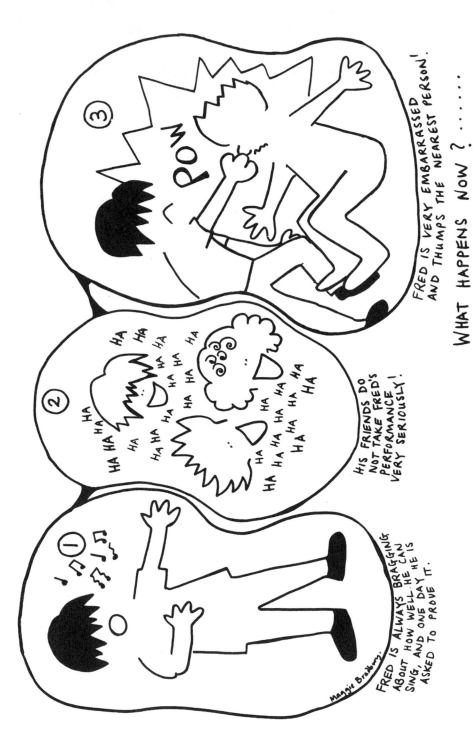

Figure 13

Activity 37

Objective: To help the class examine their self-defeating reactions to challenge, loss of face or frustration.

The form tutor introduces this activity by discussing the way in which we can retreat from challenge, or react in a way which brings trouble, when we feel we have lost face. Reference is made to the previous activity and simple illustrations given; for example, doing something we don't really want to do because somebody calls us 'chicken'; or not joining in an activity because we are afraid we cannot do it.

The groups then discuss one or two incidents that they recall. Their task is to find positive ways of behaving in these situations. After ten minutes' discussion the form tutor asks a group to volunteer to discuss their situation and the solution to it with the whole class.

Attitudes which influence performance

It is important that in these two years we help pupils examine the way they allocate responsibility for their success or failure. There are two extreme tendencies. On the one hand, they see others as responsible for their successes or failures; on the other, they accept that they themselves are the source of all that befalls them. Perhaps this sounds banal; yet the fact is that many adolescents adopt a position where the power seems to lie with others. When this happens they reject accountability for their own progress. Learning is something which happens, apparently being beyond the control of the individual.

Pressures and exhortation are of little use with pupils who take this position. Indeed, they seem to boomerang, reinforcing the passivity they are intended to change. The argument here is that in these two years we should begin to teach pupils about these processes. Without knowledge of them they are handicapped. This teaching must reflect the basic principle that we must use the concrete and familiar as starting points. Equally, there must be no impression of attack or blame if the passive pupils are to discard their defences against learning. Activities such as those which follow incorporate these principles.

Activity 38

Objective: To stimulate awareness of the tendency to blame others when one experiences failure; and to examine the validity of this mechanism.

A tape is prepared in which two girls are heard talking. One has done badly in a test and the other has done well. The former launches herself into a flood of excuses, blaming others for her failure. She might, for example, blame her friends, saying that she had to go out with them. If she did not, they would reject her. The friend interrupts this evasive process, pointing out – in a humorous and not pious way – that she, in fact, shares some of those friends, yet they did not drop her. More than this, she also has a Saturday job which the other girl does not. What then is the reason for her success? She begins to help her friend by discussing self-management and using time efficiently.

The small groups then discuss:

a the tendency to blame others;

b the principles of using time effectively.

At the end of the period, the form tutor structures the discussion around methods of using time efficiently.

Activity 39

Objectives: (a) To allow pupils to examine their defences against work; (b) To analyse the way they use their time.

(N.B. For obvious reasons this activity should not be used on a Monday.)

The teacher writes the following statement on the blackboard:

If you did all they expect you to do, you would have no time for anything else!

The class is given two minutes to discuss this.

Then duplicated sheets are handed out, divided into all the hours of the day. Pupils are then asked to write in for each hour of yesterday what they did. It is suggested that they look at:

– time spent in eating and drinking;

– enjoying themselves;

– sleeping;

– working;

– just drifting – doing nothing much.

The form tutor then opens a discussion on self-management. He gets the class to produce more of the evasive statements – for example, 'I would work if only my parents didn't nag so.' The session ends by drawing together ideas for using time more effectively.

Activity 40

Objectives: (a) To help pupils to examine the reasons for a recent success or failure; (b) To introduce the possibility of support from friends in modifying behaviour.

In small groups of four or with partners, pupils discuss their marks in a recent test. They look for the reasons for their success or relative failure. Next, they discuss what supports they could give one another.

The form tutor may follow up the discussion directly or consolidate earlier work on revision or preparing for a test.

Activity 41
Objective: To help pupils cope with a common problem, 'catching up' with work after an absence.
The problem is described:

A pupil has been absent for a fortnight due to sickness. He/she now has to decide how to catch up on the missed work.

The tutor initiates the discussion, exploring:
a what *must* be dealt with and what can be left. The level of risk in such decisions should be made clear;
b the strategies used: merely 'copying up' from friends' books; working through homework assignments; consultation with teachers.

Discussion in small groups then follows. Pupils examine how they coped when it happened to them.

In the final discussion, the form tutor pays special attention to the linear or step-by-step subjects such as physics or mathematics. He also suggests that pupils approach the subject teacher as soon as possible in those circumstances.

Activity 42
Objective: To introduce the comparison process and encourage pupils to use it constructively.
Comparison of oneself with others is strong in adolescence. Most pupils dislike being different from their peers and constantly scan to ensure that they fit the norm. Under stress, people tend to make comparisons of a negative type, for example, 'I'm the only one who has this difficulty.' But comparisons can be very productive at times.

The tutor introduces the topic by pointing out that we can learn the skills of successful working from one another. He asks the pupils to think of someone *they like* whom they also see as a success. They are then asked to write down the key words which show why they are a success. The pupils then decide what they could usefully adopt from the attitudes and behaviour of that person. Small group discussion follows.

This can be extended by careful selection of a pupil from the year above who is a competent worker. It is explained to him that the class will wish to ask him questions about the way he studies and works. The form should spend a little time formulating questions before he comes in, allowing the session to start on target and with vigour. At the end the form tutor comments positively on the experience.

(A number of variations on this activity will quickly suggest themselves to the form tutor. This activity indicates just one way in which we can use pupils as resources in pastoral care.)

Difficulties in these guidance activities are feared by those unused to them. One safeguard is always to give the objectives of the activity as advocated in the first chapter. As teachers we are vulnerable when our pupils say, 'I don't see the point of this'. If they say, 'That's silly', we recoil in confusion. As good teachers we anticipate such reactions by telling them the point of the activity so that they are correctly orientated to it. Where attainment is visibly valued and rewarded by the total staff, then guidance for success is readily accepted as legitimate by the pupils. Rutter *et al.* (1979) showed that emphasis on homework was associated with better outcomes. They argue that homework is of symbolic importance in underlining the school's concern with academic progress. This writer is convinced from experience with individuals and groups that prolonged concern with study skills and the development of learning styles has an added positive effect on outcomes. But (it cannot be stressed too often) the effort must be consistent and be shared among the majority of staff. Schools are full of sporadic onslaughts – pupils learn merely that they *are* short-lived if we are not careful.

Creating awareness of an individual learning style
It is not too early in these middle years to stimulate consciousness of individual preferences in learning. Indeed, as this is the age when identity begins to be shaped, omitting the development of a learning style is short-sighted. Failure to pay attention to it may give rise to the incomplete adult for whom learning is an alien activity. We often feel that sparkle deserts many pupils during their progress through the secondary school. Could this tendency be accentuated by our failure to relate learning to personality at a critical stage?

The methods are simple and economical. In the first year we discussed self-management and the structuring of homework. Attention now turns to individual differences in the span of time which provides maximum return for individuals. The style of revision for terminal examinations which they find rewarding and the conditions under which they learn best should be explored. The tutor will not suggest there is one way which leads to success and must be adopted. It is made clear to pupils that discovery of the conditions in which they learn well is part of the responsibility of becoming adult.

Activity 43
Objective: To make pupils aware of their preferences for learning particular things at different times of the day.

The form tutor initiates the activity by drawing attention to the idea that people have different times of the day when they can study efficiently. There may be times when the individual can take in facts, read or write essays more efficiently. To discover these things is to be more in charge of oneself.

Groups of three pupils then discuss the best time for them to do the things mentioned above. They are asked to:
a   try and explain why they think this occurs;
b   look at any difficulties associated with particular times for undertaking certain activities.

One pupil in the group then discusses the reasons for his choice, while the others challenge him by suggesting snags or pointing out difficulties he seems to be ignoring. They then give positive advice.

Note that the challenge should only occur in the small informal group. To put an individual in front of the class could be intimidating for some, while it might cause others to cling obstinately to their position even though it was unhelpful to them.

A general discussion follows in which the form tutor writes the main points up on the blackboard. He should emphasize in this summary the desirability of thinking about when one learns best.

Activity 44
Objectives: (a) To focus attention on different ways of tackling revision for examinations; (b) To allow pupils to experiment with the method they think they would prefer.

The tutor presents the class with the situation in which a pupil wishes to revise for the terminal examinations each night for a week. He realizes he has a number of decisions to make:

- whether he will study without a break for the whole two hours.
- if he has breaks how many will there be?
- how long will each break be?
- will all the periods of learning be of equal lengths? If not, which will be longer and why?

A short audiotape is presented in which two boys are heard discussing their strategies. One likes to split his two hours into three periods with the longest one in the middle. The other says he finds it better to have his first period as the longer of two periods. They also mention the fact that they always end by ten minutes spent in testing themselves: one uses a tape recorder on which he records what he recalls. The other uses a diagram.

Small groups discuss what they think would be best for them. They then split into pairs and explain why they think this is so to one another.

The tutor ends by suggesting that they try out their method that evening and report back what happened in the next tutor period – hopefully the following day.

This activity is obviously best introduced about ten days before revision proper begins.

Activity 45
Objective: To allow pupils to explore their preferences for revising.
The form tutor points out that it is profitable to ask oneself questions about what approaches to learning yield the best results. There is no single 'right way'. This is as true for revision as for any other activity. In his introductory talk, which should be brief, the tutor suggests that the salient questions are concerned with:

1 *the number of subjects revised in one block of time.*
   (Some people find it more useful to concentrate on a single subject for two hours, and others find they do better if they revise several subjects.)

2 *the spacing of revisions.*
   (This looks at the concept of distributed learning and should create awareness of the need to revise at intervals. Pupils can

have their attention drawn to the rapid drop-off in memory and the implication of this.)

Pupils discuss this in small groups. They are asked to look carefully at:

a The reasons for their choice of strategy.

b Any costs and consequences attached to their chosen procedure.

In the final section of this guidance period the tutor asks for three volunteers to discuss their decisions. He writes any particularly good points on the board. The class is asked to try their strategy out for a week and then report back.

Activity 46

Objective: To alert pupils to the possibility of mutual help between friends.

The tutor points out that it is sensible for friends to work together and help one another succeed. He then asks, 'How could this be done?' Pupils provide ideas which are put on the blackboard.

Pupils are then given a sheet of paper on which the following appears:

THINGS I NEED TO DO TO GET GOOD RESULTS	THE STEPS I WILL TAKE	HOW MY FRIEND WILL HELP ME

When this is filled in, the form tutor draws attention to the need to be very specific about the steps and the ways in which friends help one another. The class is asked to try this for a week and then discuss the results in a tutor period.

Activity 47

Objective: To place pupils in a position where they have to compare someone else's revision strategy with their own.

A tape recording is presented to the form in which a pupil is heard describing his methods of revising for terminal examinations. Care must be taken to ensure that he does not come across as either a paragon of virtue or an insufferable prig. He must

appear lively and competent. His techniques could include:
- the policy of following up a first revision by a second within 24 hours and then leaving it for a week;
- building a set of cards: on one side is a diagram which contains the key points which have to be remembered, on the reverse are conventional notes;
- he works on two subjects each evening, having split his revision by a proper break in the middle;
- he keeps a diary, writing down every night when he finishes what he is going to do the next night;
- he likes to try to anticipate examination questions, therefore he sets his own and does skeleton answers;
- he tests himself by using his tape recorder, checking his notes to see if he is correct;
- when he feels fed up he talks to his parents.

The tutor writes these points upon the board as they are presented. Alternatively, a transparency can be prepared in advance.

The form discusses the tape in small groups, comparing it with their own techniques of revising for the examination.

The form tutor then asks the pupils to see if there is anything they could usefully adopt in their own revision.

Activity 48
Objectives: (a) To provide experience of decision-making which allows pupils to make use of what has been explored above; (b) To provide evaluation from a peer.

The form is divided into groups of five. Each situation will be discussed for 15 minutes by four of the group. They will try to reach a decision. After this, the fifth member attempts to evaluate the decision they have made. Help is given to this peer judge by a transparency (Fig 14).

Each member of the group has the opportunity of being the judge as there are five situations, each of which occupies a period. The tutor, as usual, structures the ideas at the end of the tutor period.

Situations
1 Six weeks before the summer examinations a friend tells you he wants to do well but is not sure of the best way to tackle his revision. He asks you for help. What advice do you give him?

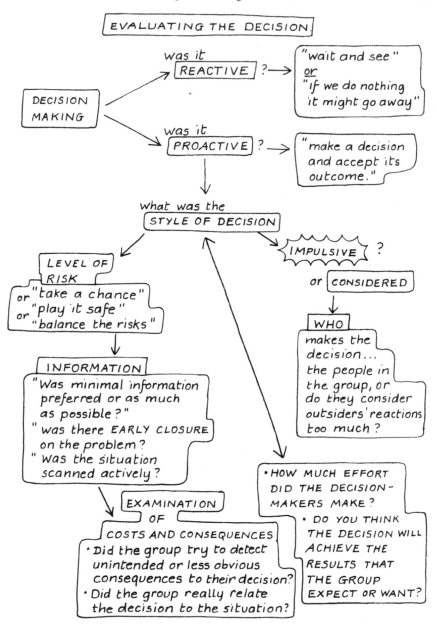

EVALUATING THE DECISION

DECISION MAKING

was it REACTIVE ? → "wait and see" or "if we do nothing it might go away"

was it PROACTIVE ? → "make a decision and accept its outcome."

what was the STYLE OF DECISION

LEVEL OF RISK
or "take a chance"
or "play it safe"
or "balance the risks"

IMPULSIVE ?
or CONSIDERED

WHO makes the decision... the people in the group, or do they consider outsiders' reactions too much ?

INFORMATION
"Was minimal information preferred or as much as possible?"
" was there EARLY CLOSURE on the problem?
" was the situation scanned actively ?

EXAMINATION OF COSTS AND CONSEQUENCES
· Did the group try to detect unintended or less obvious consequences to their decision?
· Did the group really relate the decision to the situation?

· HOW MUCH EFFORT DID THE DECISION-MAKERS MAKE ?
· DO YOU THINK THE DECISION WILL ACHIEVE THE RESULTS THAT THE GROUP EXPECT OR WANT?

Figure 14

2 Your best friend says he feels absolutely fed up because he thinks he will do badly in the examinations. He says there is no point in studying. What do you do about this?
3 If someone of your age finds he cannot remember what he reads, what should he do?

4 The teacher has asked you to give a talk to another class on 'How to Study'. What would you include?

5 A new boy or girl says 'I don't see any sense in these study skills. I know how to study already.' What would you say to this? Why?

Consolidating and extending skills

Key points and phrases were given prominence in the training in listening, and in the diagrams advocated as a means of recall, in the earlier study skills. In the presentation of homework, the use of capital letters to bring out salient points was emphasized. These things have prepared the ground for training in effective note-taking, which should be carried out by forms in the third and fourth years.

Activity 49

Objective: To introduce pupils to making more formal notes.

Pupils are reminded of the key elements through the following diagram:

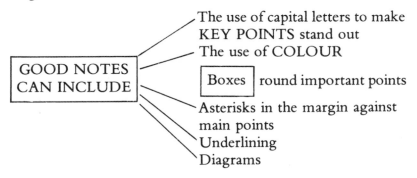

An example of layout is given to the pupils. The tutor tells pupils this is not intended as a model to be reproduced blindly, but as the point of departure for making their own notes. One such example is given in Fig 15.

Pupils then discuss what they find helpful in the model and are encouraged to modify it as they think best.

The tutor then gives a ten minute talk which provides the material for pupils' note-taking.

At the end, pupils assess their effort after discussing it with a friend.

University students can do badly in their examinations because they fail to plan and structure their answers. Whether or not one

<u>Notes on the Feudal System</u>.

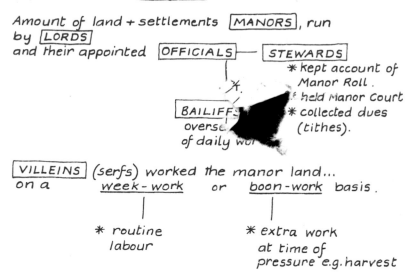

Amount of land + settlements [MANORS], run
by [LORDS]
and their appointed [OFFICIALS]——[STEWARDS]
* kept account of
Manor Roll.
* held Manor Court
[BAILIFFS] * collected dues
oversee (tithes).
of daily wor

[VILLEINS] (serfs) worked the manor land...
on a   week-work   or   boon-work basis.

* routine   * extra work
labour   at time of
                 pressure e.g. harvest

<u>Villeins</u> could have their own STRIPS of land
in OPEN FIELD system, + grow own crops
near dwellings.
Certain dues or <u>tithes</u> were payable to the Lord
of the Manor via the Steward. These were in
recordings on the Manor Roll.
    e.g.   * provisions at festival times.
            * part of strip or home grown crops.
            * fees for grinding corn.

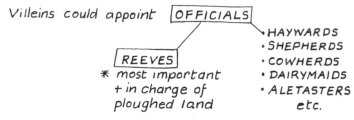

Villeins could appoint [OFFICIALS]

                              •HAYWARDS
                              •SHEPHERDS
[REEVES]   •COWHERDS
* most important   •DAIRYMAIDS
+ in charge of   •ALETASTERS
ploughed land   etc.

Figure 15

would predict that any particular pupils will proceed to tertiary
education, they need help with study skills in the third and fourth
years. If they can detect the headlines under which other facts can
be subsumed, arranging the headlines in a logical sequence, then
the subsidiary facts and ideas will be relevant. Pupils can be
encouraged to plan carefully the outline of an essay before they
begin writing. The following provides a first step.

Essay structure

1   *The introduction*
This states the main points and arguments briefly, indicating the rationale which shapes the essay.

2   *The main exposition*
Broken down into:

Major theme one — subsidiary facts and arguments / ideas and questions

Major theme two — subsidiary facts and arguments / ideas and questions

Major theme three — subsidiary facts and arguments / ideas and questions

3   *Conclusion* — recapitulation / balanced appraisal

Activity 50
Objective: To give experience of structuring an essay or answer to a question, using the framework above.
Pupils are presented with one of the following topics:

    a   'The school leaving age should be raised by a year in this age of unemployment.' Assess this statement.

    b   'Girls should have woodwork and metalwork and boys should have cookery and home economics included in their subjects.' Explain why you agree or disagree with this point of view.

A spider, family tree or flow diagram is used to bring out the main themes and subsidiary facts, ideas or questions. The pupil then creates a 'skeleton' essay following the structure suggested.

In the final class discussion the form tutor collects ideas from the class for improving the plan.

Activity 51
Objective: To give added practice in making skeleton answers and examining the meaning of a question.
Pupils may possess a stock of ideas and yet lack the capacity to organize them into a coherent whole.

The following is presented:

Violence on television is responsible for the growth of aggressive behaviour in Britain today. Carefully evaluate this statement.

The exercise is developed as follows:

a Pupils are given five minutes to discuss the exact meaning of this question. Attention is drawn to the key verb. (This can be partner work.)

b The form then works in groups of four to build up a stock of ideas which can be used. Twelve minutes should be sufficient.

c Each pupil then plans his skeleton answer using the framework on page 90 (see Fig 16 for example).

d A final discussion pays attention to the importance of a workmanlike conclusion which leaves the reader with a sense of the writer's competence.

Exploring anxiety and developing coping strategies

For the present, in considering anxiety, we will take the simple view that anxiety is a signal of danger. This idea underlies the work of Lazarus (1966). Unfortunately, the reaction to the threat can be less than constructive. Pupils react to anxiety about tests by avoidance, self-defeating forms of learning or defensive rejection of the possibility of success. The fourth year provides the ideal time for discussion of some of the manifestations of anxiety as a preparatory step for the programme which deals with the stresses of public examinations in the fifth year.

The following activities break into habitual responses in a helpful way, provided that the form tutor introduces them at the relevant moment. To wait until the terminal examination is imminent, and then introduce them, is to invite their rejection. Conscientious or anxious pupils will find a change in revision strategies disruptive and alarming. Those who have indulged in defensive withdrawal will be committed to their position. Too early an introduction before there is recognition of the need to revise, obviously reduces their impact. The point of intervention is therefore a crucial element to which the head of year and form tutor must pay attention. If the original approaches continue, underfunctioning will be reinforced. Precision in the sense of calling attention to mechanisms just before they begin to operate can lead to growth and improved functioning. Exhortation is sterile, but the awareness stemming from active exploration can be productive.

Activity 52

Objectives: (a) To help pupils examine reactions to examinations

<u>ESSAY</u>.

"VIOLENCE ON T.V. IS RESPONSIBLE FOR THE GROWTH
OF AGGRESSIVE BEHAVIOUR IN BRITAIN TODAY."
Carefully evaluate this statement.

I <u>Introduction</u>.
   T.V. plays large part in promotion of violence.
   Other forms of media also responsible.
   Root cause may be rapid changes within society.

II <u>Exposition</u>.
   (1.) Power of T.V. as media form. (T.V. LARGELY RESPONSIBLE)
       ⓐ system for mass communication to vulnerable
          audiences.
       ⓑ sound, VISION (colour) of violent events.
       ⓒ presents <u>actual</u> + <u>fictional</u> violence, DAILY—
          local, national + international settings.
       ⓓ uses heroes/anti-heroes to act out violent
          behaviour — powerful models.
   (2.) <u>but</u> other forms of media share responsibility for
       promoting violence. (T.V. NOT TO BE SCAPEGOAT)
           e.g. newspapers, books, cinema, public figures.
           T.V. is not the only source of violent images.
   (3.) Examine possible root cause.
           (T.V. NOT INITIALLY RESPONSIBLE, NOR OTHER
           MEDIA FORMS)
       ⓐ rapid changes in society pressurise individuals,
          groups.
       ⓑ familiar social structures cannot cope with
          these changes effectively.
       ⓒ individuals + groups act out frustrations
          violently.
       ⓓ models from T.V. <u>etc</u>. may reinforce violent
          behaviour but have not caused it.

III <u>Conclusion</u>.
       Considering arguments in II ③ suggest that T.V.
       (amongst others) is a means of communication
       exploited by society which created it. The society
       is responsible for violence <u>but</u> T.V. helps its
       expression of violence.
       Perhaps suggest means of further change to
       alternative behaviours — e.g. <u>via</u> education.

Figure 16

which may be the product of anxiety; (b) To allow them to explore other ways of behaving which are more productive.

The following duplicated sheet is distributed and pupils are asked to think about the seven questions it contains.

FEELINGS ABOUT EXAMINATIONS

What to do

a Please tick the box which is most like the way you feel.

b When you have done this, your tutor will tell you how to use the ideas underneath each questions.

1 When I am preparing for an exam I get the feeling I will never remember the answers.

LIKE ME	NOT LIKE ME

What can you do? — Test yourself by using diagrams or or a tape recorder.
— Try some skeleton answers to questions.

2 I worry about how well I will do in the exam, and then I can't get started on my revision.

LIKE ME	NOT LIKE ME

What can you do? — Write down each night when you finish revising what you will tackle the next night.
— Try and do a skeleton answer every evening.

3 When I have the test my mind goes blank and I find it hard to start writing.

LIKE ME	NOT LIKE ME

What can you do? — Look for an easy question and begin to write down key points.
— Read through the paper and work out the order in which you will tackle the questions.

4 I try to learn everything off by heart and then end up worrying because I feel it is impossible.

LIKE ME	NOT LIKE ME

What can you do? — Look for the key points and put them on a card as a diagram.
— Say I must remember the really important things and concentrate on them.

5	I know I really can answer the questions, yet somehow I can't put it down on paper.	LIKE ME	NOT LIKE ME

What can you do? —Build up my skills of planning by making skeleton answers.
—Always jot down the three or four key facts before I begin to write.

6	I work for so long the nights before the test that I feel tired out or just don't care how I do.	LIKE ME	NOT LIKE ME

What can you do? —Discuss my feelings with the form tutor or my parents.
—Make a plan for study times which lets me relax and have enough sleep.

7	When I don't like the subject I expect to do badly.	LIKE ME	NOT LIKE ME

What can you do? —Make a balance sheet of how you will allocate your time, making sure that you are not neglecting this subject.
—Begin to ask yourself why you feel like this and, if you can, change your feelings.

The form tutor then points out to the form that the suggestions are only 'starter ideas', and that therefore they must provide their own solutions. It is important that after the administration of the questionnaire the pupils are allowed to discuss any points freely. At the close of the class discussion the tutor should get pupils to rank the seven items in order of importance for them. The results should be tabulated by the tutor. In the next tutorial period this ranking should be discussed, the top three items being fully explored in later guidance sessions. It is helpful if pupils can see the table on the blackboard.

Activity 53
Objective: To help pupils discuss and evaluate responses to anxiety and predictions of failure.
(This activity is based on Bradbury (1981) who devised the

game STOP, WAIT and GO which gives the framework for exploration of the consequences of behaviour.)

1 STOP! Each small group is given the following card:

> **STOP!**
> You are very worried about the end of the year exams. You are afraid that your parents will be hurt and disappointed at your results. An added worry is that your friends are doing well and they also expect you to do well.

Six minutes is allowed to discuss the significance of this situation.

2 WAIT! The next card offers three possible reactions and there is room for the groups to work out their own suggestion.

> **WAIT!**
> 1. You begin to tell your friends you are doing badly.
> 2. You start to invent excuses for doing badly.
> 3. You wait for your teachers and your parents to *make* you work.
> 4. . . . .
>   . . . .

3 GO! The GO! card is accompanied by slips of paper on which individuals write their own idea of a solution before general group discussion. In the group discussion, differences of perspective are examined, but although members are required to justify their position, the tutor does not insist that a uniform decision is made in each small group.

4 In the final form discussion the tutor calls attention to:
  a the reasons why people work, mentioning the dangers of

working only to please others and the need to pursue success actively;

b the costs and consequences of strategies which savour of
evasion or anticipate failure.

Activity 54

Objective: *To inoculate pupils against the negative aspects of pressure.*
This writer has found that the simple device of mini-exams in
which pupils are required to work at pressure, planning and
writing brief answers, helps pupils cope with tensions and pressure. They are usually pleasantly surprised to discover how
much they can produce.

In a 35-minute period, pupils are presented with three general
questions. They are then required to spend 2–3 minutes in planning their answers. After this, they are allowed 7–8 minutes to
write an outline answer. The timing is kept in their hands,
although the tutor should ensure that they can see a clock or
timer.

A brief discussion follows on the importance of timing and
getting to the salient points.

What other activities would be useful?

Study skills are concerned with mastering demands and eventually
autonomy. Tools should be made available to pupils on demand.
One such tool is a set of tapes which bring out the elements of a
problem and suggest solutions in an informal context. Beaumont
(1976) reports on the effectiveness of such tapes, but unfortunately
details of the content are scanty. Teachers may find it difficult to
make such a tape without some guide. The examples which follow
are largely derived from the work of Maggie Bradbury.

Space prohibits the presentation of more than two examples.
Language and content can be varied to fit the age, intelligence and
current demands on the pupil. What follows is intended for the
unmotivated fourth year pupil. In the first tape the way in which
an interest can be used to teach the skill of structuring an essay is
enlightening.

STUDY SKILL TAPE : ESSAY WRITING

T = Teacher : P = Pupil

T *What seems to hold you up on essay writing?*

P Well, I don't know – sometimes when I see a title, I get so many ideas from it I don't know which one to use, or how to start it off. I think starting it off is the main problem. Once I've started I feel a bit better, but then sometimes I change my mind once I've started off, and everything gets into a muddle. I'm often put off by titles, too. If I don't like a title I can't even think straight.

T *Maybe it's something to do with how you organize your ideas. Let's work on an example together. I'll be a sort of reporter and take down your ideas and we'll see what happens.*

P What's the topic? Something corny like 'My Hobby' really turns me off.

T *What is one of your main interests at the moment? Let's use a topic which you have lots of ideas about, and see if you can get control of all your ideas. There's a challenge!*

P My main interest is pop music – is that all right for an essay?

T *Well, you've probably got quite a few strong opinions about it, and background knowledge. You can organize your ideas in the essay to put across your interest – you'll then get others interested too!*

P What shall I say? How can I start?

T *What about starting off with a personal statement? Why do you like it?*

P Well, it's alive, up-to-date. I like groups, some of the fashions they wear, I like some singers on their own, but mainly groups. I really like loud numbers – I like 'The Draft' best at the moment – they're really good – they remind me of reggae music, and they're a bit like 'Full Moon' and –––

T *Phew! Hold it! My hand's going to seize up! You're saying a lot here – some great materials to work on. Let me read it back to you.*
 ALIVE – UP-TO-DATE – GROUPS (REASONS FOR LIKING) – INDIVIDUALS (REASONS FOR LIKING) – TYPE OF MUSIC AND PERFORMANCES – SPECIAL GROUPS (REASONS FOR LIKING)
 We can put this into some order for you so you can make a go of writing your essay.

P Did I say all that?

T *Yes. How can we organize it? What will you start off with?*

P Why I like pop music – oh, and why some people don't.

T *Yes. First part: your own reasons for appreciating it, and reasons why others might not.*

P Yes – that's the first two paragraphs.

T *Any snags?*

P I suppose I've got to watch out for slamming into people who don't like it. I might get too outspoken.

T *I think you're talking about being one-sided, and not seeing the other people's point of view. Perhaps it is a good idea to state an alternative viewpoint clearly without agreeing or disagreeing too heavily with it. Take a balanced look at the situation.*

P Well, if my first part is about why I like it and some don't – what about the second?

T *What about an example of a group you particularly appreciate, and the reasons why. Bring out why you like them – everything from their music to their style of performances to the clothes they wear.*

P Yes – I could do that with 'The Draft'. I'll tackle an individual singer too. That would be a sort of contrast, wouldn't it?

T *Yes. Are there any groups or individuals you don't like? That would give a contrast too. You sound as if you don't like all pop music – full stop.*

P I can't stand 'The Mugs' or people who get in the charts because everybody knows them.

T *What about a paragraph on your dislikes with some clear reasons about what you don't like – musically and performance-wise?*

P Oh, I see what you mean. I don't like the kind of songs they sing – they sound very artificial or the same as lots of others which have been going on for years.

T *Back to the 'up-to-date' point then?*

P Yes. I know 'The Draft' have a lot of reggae in their songs, but they have their own style too. I suppose it's different people having different tastes. Some people can't stand reggae, of course.

T *Right – try and talk about that. That's another personal statement, but acknowledging that others have theirs to make too, probably for very good reasons.*

P What have I got so far as the plan, then?

T *First part: Why you like pop music. Why it's your main interest. Contrasted with why some people don't. Second part: your favourite group and an example of a favourite individual singer with reasons why you like them. Third part: a contrast here. Groups and individuals you don't like with reasons why. Plus recognizing other people have different tastes and different viewpoints.*

P That sounds quite a lot – where should I go from there?

T *What about continuing to look at the wider viewpoint? You could bring in your ideas of what you think pop music does for people in general?*

P Well, I think it is a good thing. I mean it's this business of being alive – do you know even old people like pop music? It's really up-to-date and always changing. Sometimes it goes back into old music – they even use people like Beethoven. Sometimes it's rubbish, but there's some which really lasts.

T *Good point. What about that as your final argument? What makes pop music important in life today? What it does for people – whether it lasts or not. What lasts and what fades away – and your point about the changes.*

P Right. Hey, how much do I have to write?

T *You can always experiment in your first try. Make some notes for each part now we've worked on the ideas and their organization. See what comes out of it. We can always cut down or build up the result, if we need to.*

P Right. I'll come and ask if I get stuck.

T *Fine! Go and make a start now. I think you'll find you've got a lot to work on, and it's in some sort of order now.*

P Right. I'll see you later then, with some organized ideas.

This informal approach seems to be effective, probably because it links with existing ideas and associations. The tapes should stand out from other activities, stimulating the pupil to think about problems for himself. Straightforward information can be included at the conclusion of the narrative. A further example is given of a tape designed for a fifth year girl. It can, of course, be altered to suit the fourth year.

| STUDY SKILLS TAPE : |
| EXAMINATION PREPARATION |

T = *Teacher* : P = Pupil

T *You're worried about the exams?*

P Well, I don't know how to fit it all in. I've got these subjects coming up in mocks. I keep on swotting for Biology and History and nothing seems to stick. English and French are all right – I mean I know what I'm doing in them, and I can remember French vocabulary. Maths is all right for me – it's just a sit down and get on with it. But I'm just terrified of learning all those notes for History and Biology. I don't know what to do with them – there are pages and pages.

T *Do you try to revise at a particular time?*

P Well, I put in a bit of time at school – but there's music, debating society, prefect duties and I can't ignore my friends at breaks and lunchtimes. It's impossible to do revision at school. We're still taking notes.

T *Yes, I do see your difficulty. What could you do at home?*

P Well, I've got a lot on at home, but I do about two hours every night – at least I try to – but it's usually when I go to bed and I'm really tired by then and I don't seem to remember anything.

T *Let's work on this. The time you learn is important for your success. Let's pinpoint the times when it's actually possible to do some revision, whether or not you feel up to it. Shall we see what time can be made available, and then look at how to use the time?*

P Yes. First of all I can begin when I go in at a quarter past four. We don't have to do anything until mother comes in at five-thirty. It might be a good time to use the History revision notes we have been given.

T *Good. I wonder if the History notes pick out the important topics and what has to be learned?*

P Yes.

T *Then it may be a good idea to begin your study period at 4.15 p.m. by using the History notes. Then can you go on to use the same idea in Biology? Go through your books and pick out the important topics. Then make short notes of the main facts under each one – like newspaper headlines with short reports under each one. Don't forget to do your diagrams but also try to put the key points into a single pattern. That will help them stick. You might ask your teacher for help with the diagrammatic notes.*

P I hadn't thought of this way of doing it. Do you think I've got enough time or do I need to make more?

T *It is your success or failure. What do you think?*

P I ought to do more – but I must help mother. She gets worn out with the younger children and her job.

T *I like your concern. Could you now find a short time – say forty-five minutes – for extra study?*

P Yes, I could do something from about 8.15 p.m. to 9.0 p.m. But I don't think I could start on new work at that time.

T *I see, although you are keen, you do get very tired. Well, we must accept this, but not develop the feeling of failure or get depressed. I wonder what you could do?*

P Well – sometimes I like to test myself. I quite enjoy that.

T *Right – let's make a bargain – I'll keep an eye on things, but your job is to revise new material earlier in the evening, and then later on test yourself on what you did in the first part of the evening and also go over things you have revised some days before.*

P Well – that's good. I don't think I will muddle things up so easily.

T *Now let's look at it more deeply. Are you doing sample questions, using your notes, as well as straight learning off by heart?*

P We have done it in class – but it was all together.

T *How did it help?*

P Well, it was fine for History, but not so good for Biology. I'd rather learn the notes in Biology.

T *Yes – it is your decision. It does seem to be the actual learning of facts which bothers you, not writing the answers to questions.*

P Yes – I'm glad you see it. I'm good at waffling on paper, but I've got to have the facts to go on.

T *Right! We're back to your basic task. (a) Between 4.15 and 5.30 p.m. you can (i) sort out Biology notes under headings. Use diagrams as well to make the key points stand out. (ii) Revise History, using revision sheets. You will have to decide how long you spend on each subject.*

Then (b) Test yourself on what you revised earlier in the evening. You've also got to work out a plan for testing yourself at intervals on what you did earlier in the week. Use your time in school to sort out notes with the help of your teachers if you find any special difficulties.

P Do you know – I go baby-sitting on Saturday – I can take my notes then. Is daily revision a good idea?

T *I think so, provided you don't get stale. Try it and see. Discuss your feelings about it with your form tutor.*

These two examples merely illustrate one approach. Teachers may prefer a more directly didactic method accompanied by exercises undertaken after listening to the tape. The material offered in this chapter can be adapted for this purpose quite easily.

4: The Fifth Year

CONSTRAINTS OF FIFTH YEAR GUIDANCE

The fact that the fifth year is a critical point in the academic and career prospects of the student imposes constraints on the form and amount of guidance that can be proffered. Students who have accepted the validity of school values and have a sense of direction perceive success in the fifth year as vital to guarantee the opportunity to strive for future achievements. O-Levels are believed to – and do to some extent – function as a regulator which opens or closes doors to life goals. Awareness of examinations, as a form of evaluation which will determine whether they merit the benefits of further educational qualifications or whether they should disengage from their pursuit, creates a sense of pressure. In turn, this can produce a rigidity and insecurity which narrows their openness to new methods and new ideas. To attempt to impose any drastic changes in the methods of study a few months before the examinations would be imperceptive. Panic would be produced in the sensitive student. The hard-boiled student's response would be that of denying our credibility and actively rejecting us as a source of influence. By the fifth year the student has developed a characteristic way of organizing and processing information. Violation of this by attempting to impose a uniform pattern of study would be destructive.

We have seen the advantages of systematic introduction of study skills in the early years of the secondary school. Therefore, if possible, fifth year work should rest on, and then extend what has been done earlier. Before proceeding further, it is necessary to explain the omissions in this book. This writer has dealt with the mechanics of study skills for this age group in earlier publications (Hamblin, 1978, 1981); and readers would find it useful to consult them.

Three closely related areas – possibly overlapping ones – can be detected which should be given salience in the tutorial periods preceding the mock examinations:

1 Self-management, self-evaluation and self-diagnosis.
2 The reinforcement and extension of learning behaviours which are productive for the individual.
3 Tension management and copying with parental and self-imposed pressures.

Passive reliance upon the teacher contravenes the basic principle of pastoral care that the objective is to help the pupil develop controls from within and take responsibility for what befalls him. It would be too tough-minded to regard anxiety as self-indulgent behaviour because it directs attention to feelings and the self rather than to task achievement. But guidance has to stimulate constructive coping behaviour and give pupils the opportunity to evaluate their work. Effective fifth year guidance therefore builds up the pupil's capacity to analyse his strengths and weaknesses as a learner and then do something about them. Realism demands that the form tutor guards against analysis which is not followed by action. Students can develop an awareness of what strengths could be built on and what deficiencies have to be dealt with, but still fail to make a change.

The tutor will be striving to increase self-respect as this is linked with responsible behaviour, as Rosenberg (1965) shows. We must not, however, over-simplify the situation. Study skill techniques and tutorial work may not have only beneficial effects. They can boost the confidence of those who are nervous or undervalue themselves, but reduce it in the arrogant and imperceptive by creating awareness of limitations and defects. Ambiguities exist in the interpretation of research into the self-concept, as Wylie (1961) shows. Despite this, fifth year guidance will be concerned with the ideal towards which students strive, and their perceptions of where they stand in relation to it. Where a large discrepancy exists between the ideal and the actual selves, the sense of competence built up through the supportive structure of tutorial work can reduce the abortive, almost self-punitive immersion in unproductive forms of study. Inroads into the complacency of those who have a low level of aspiration, and whose ideal self has apparently been achieved, occur as they learn about themselves with healthy results.

We should not see a discrepancy between the ideal and actual self as necessarily harmful. It helps to stimulate striving; indeed, as Katz and Zigler (1967) show, the discrepancy increases with age, reaching its peak at sixteen. Again, we must note the difficulty of interpreting the meaning of such a disparity, for what is stimulating in one individual is an oppressive burden to another. The head of year or house has to alert tutors to these considerations, perhaps encouraging them to concentrate on that area of the self-concept concerned with the perceptions held by the student of himself as a learner. At the forefront of this will be predictions about future success and the outcomes of study.

The aim of guidance in this year is two-fold: to anticipate difficulties, and then to inoculate them against unavoidable stress by facing facts squarely. Perhaps we can delude ourselves. It is desirable and essential that pupils should have confidence in their teachers, but as O'Shea (1980) demonstrated, having confidence in the teacher does not reduce examination anxiety even in the teacher's subject area. Easy reassurances or blind attempts to restore belief in self can be counter-productive. We may be trapped into what I call 'scorpion' communication – that is, with a sting in the tail! 'I think you will do quite well in the exams, John. But don't worry if you do fail, there is always another chance in November.' The student who is alert to negative cues reacts to the latter statement, leaving the teacher puzzled that the kindly re-assurance does not work. Banal, when set out baldly as above, and yet it happens all too often.

Students need a chance to look at situations in depth. Casual re-assurance can be collusion with anxiety or evasion. Fifth year form tutors need to develop skills of counselling, especially the skill of sending signals that they understand, and accept the feelings of the pupil. This is not sentimental; rather it is efficient. Beginning a discussion with statements which show one has seen matters from the pupil's perspective is crucial if there is to be meaningful communication rather than sterility or a retreat to defensive denial of problems and feeling. In recent interviews this writer recalls making the following statements early in the interaction: 'Success in this subject is very vital to your plans – the doubts you've just expressed must be worrying you deeply,' or, 'Yes, I can see you are feeling confused about the results of your Mocks.' Because they were based on the reality of the situation, they created the climate of safety. In our guidance activities in the fifth year we need to watch our use of such phrases as 'Yes, but . . . .' Students under stress interpret this as rejection, although to us it is merely a figure of speech. The student's sensitivity causes him to see this as indicating that we are not accepting his perspective, and that we intend to ladle out well-meaning advice – and all too often he is right.

Techniques of revision and help with study will be effective only when set in the climate of understanding built by the tutor who understands the processes of attribution, anxiety, denial and doubt that lurk under the surface reactions of some pupils. In-service training given by the head of house or year must begin with counselling skills.

STRUCTURING READING SKILLS

The prospect of evaluation through the examinations can build up a sense of oppression and powerlessness which erodes competence. This is often focused on the twin activities of reading and memorization, and expressed in the complaints, 'I can't read fast enough' and 'I don't seem to take in what I read.' Robinson's (1970) SQ3R, which was described in the first chapter, can be developed further. The first step might be a session based on the following duplicated sheet.

Activity 55
Students are given a duplicated sheet headed:

USING A BOOK EFFICIENTLY
In preparing for examinations we can read efficiently, or we may be wasting time. Other people may seem to do better than us, yet we can be working very hard. We may not see that the reason lies in our reading skills. When this happens we can say we are not good enough or we haven't got the ability, and quite falsely label ourselves as failures.

As a mature person your first step is to examine the way you approach learning tasks and decide whether or not you are efficient. The first step is to imagine you have been given an assignment which requires you to read a book and then use what you have read in the assignment. How would you approach it? Make notes in the space below:

Next, compare your ideas with the person sitting next to you. Now consider the diagram on the back of this sheet and discuss it with your neighbour. We are going to use this method in tutor periods.

EFFECTIVE READING

The steps you can take are set out below:

1 SCAN AND SURVEY	Look at the contents page. Quickly read the introduction. Find out if there is a summary chapter: if so, skim through it to get an idea of the main ideas in the book.
2 SEARCH	Ask why you are reading it. What is the reason for the choice of this book? A good reader extracts what he wants from a book in the minimum amount of time.
3 ORIENTATE YOURSELF	Before you begin to read the chapters or sections skim through them. Begin by reading the summary if there is one and look at the sub-headings. This allows you to orientate yourself in a way which highlights the relevant.
4 READ ACTIVELY	Extract the key points as you read. Write them down as concisely as possible. If questions come into your mind make a note of them. As soon as you finish a section, test yourself to see how much you can remember.
5 DEVELOP YOUR IDEAS	You must remember what the writer said – the facts are crucial. But you should try to develop any ideas you have about the topic and make a note of them.

The discussion is helpful but it needs to be backed by training. A week's tutor periods could be given over to intensive practice of reading skills as outlined above. Pupils would select a textbook and work to this end.

The format might be in a 20-minute period.

2 minutes to get an idea of what the passage is about;

2 minutes to raise questions about the topic;

10 minutes to read, making notes of key phrases;

6 minutes for recall activities – diagrams, notes or partner work.

This writer has found this approach very useful, but it needs considerable practice and the feeling of intensity and effort must be brought out. Done in a half-hearted way, the activity loses its impact.

Recall and memorization are key problems for the fifth year student taking examinations. To attempt to deal with them without seeing their connection with inadequate reading habits is to deal with a symptom rather than the cause. As Activity 55 suggests, students need to be trained to think about the kind of information they wish to extract. In our guidance work we have found that many fifth year pupils approach their reading tasks haphazardly, failing to orientate themselves to it with precision. Many never ask if they are gathering facts for immediate use or for later on. A sense of being in control is to train them to ask themselves, 'What do I want to get from this text or chapter?' Tutors could follow the initial training just described by help with the processing of what is read. This stage can be introduced with the following activity.

Activity 56
The class is presented with this duplicated study aid.

READING SKILLS
Recall of what you have read is essential. The following points will be of help.
  1 Write down *key ideas* and *phrases* as you read, rather than copying whole sentences or paragraphs.
  2 Look closely at the *topic sentence* which introduces each paragraph. This is especially necessary when the paragraph is a long one.
  3. Be alert to cues and *signals* which demand that you should pay special attention. Examples are: 'to summarize what I have said'; 'therefore'; 'the main point we should keep in mind'; 'this means'. Paying attention to the paragraphs in which such signals occur can be very profitable.
  4 Look very closely at the *conclusions* reached by the writer.
  5 Immediately *test* yourself and arrange your key ideas and phrases into notes or a diagram.

The activity would consist of identifying cues and signals in textbooks currently used by the students. List are made, and then their precise significance is discussed with a partner. Sensitivity to signal words must be fostered if students are to assimilate material without over-simplifying or missing the significance of the writer's qualifications and riders.

Many fifth year pupils are content if they read the text conscientiously without further processing of the material. It is necessary to teach them to distinguish between key words and phrases and the signal words and phrases. Some experience can be given of flow diagrams which encourage students to manipulate and organize their reading.

Activity 57
Reading is undertaken and then students are asked to construct a flow diagram which outlines:

    1 The main themes in logical order.
    2 Expansion of them, giving:
      a specific facts;
      b illustrative examples.
    3 Examination of the main themes, looking for:
      a their significance and importance;
      b applications of them;
      c qualifications and limits.
    Once this has been done, students search the text for related and omitted facts. These are then inserted into the diagram.

It is well known that if you wish to find out how well you have understood something, you should try and teach it to someone else. In extending the skills of reading at this level, it is useful to train students to undertake an explanatory conversation with a partner immediately after reading. The listener is not passive. He is encouraged to ask questions after the exposition and share ideas. With those whose level of achievement motivation is high I have found that this can be used as a revision device. The conversation takes place between the student and his tape recorder. The recording is played back and the student evaluates his performance and raises questions. This leads the determined actively to search out new facts, meanings and implications from the text. Reading should be a silent conversation, and such simple techniques help students read for ideas and not words.

    Heads of year or house must be prepared to support tutors as they may be unaccustomed to analysing learning activities, and feel insecure even in this aspect of pastoral care which is directly related to their teaching function. Pupils feel just the same; therefore continuous discussion between the head of year and his team of tutors is vital. If we actually think about the way we walk downstairs or shave, while we perform these activities, a broken neck or a slashed face may result because the movements have become automatic and conditioned. By the age of fifteen, reading has become an almost automatic habit taken for granted by the student. Yet they would derive great benefit from monitoring their reading, evaluating their strengths and weaknesses. Indirect approaches have seemed useful as a first step.

Activity 58
Pupils are given this sheet:

READING DIFFICULTIES
Here are some statements about reading skills in the fifth year from pupils taking examinations.
  1 I read quickly, but can't remember much when I have completed the reading.
  2 I read carefully and can remember what I've read, but I never have time to finish it.
  3 I often find it hard to distinguish what is important from what is not.
  4 Once I finish the set reading I get on with something else straight away. I then find I don't know as much about the reading as I thought I did.
  5 It is surprising how often my notes on my reading don't make much sense to me when I go back to them.
NOW Take one of those comments which interests you and make four to six suggestions which would allow the speaker to change things for the better.
NEXT Detect some aspect of reading in which you would like to improve and share some ideas about it with the person next to you.

One aspect of self-diagnosis is observation of the self as a reader. Watson and Tharp (1972) in their discussion of behaviour modification emphasize the part played by self-observation. Coupled with the individual's recording of his own behaviour, it is an important element in self-management, as Thoresen and Mahoney (1974) demonstrate. It helps pupils realize that what they stressed as a source of worry was less frequent than they believed. This helped to make the problem appear more manageable. The tutor must help the form understand that self-observation is a necessary prelude to control of behaviour. This is another instance of the need to give the objectives of an activity to the group.

Pupils can be asked to describe themselves as readers, examining both the mechanics of reading and the use they make of what has been read. A diary can be kept. Monitoring can take place during the day, pupils making entries at the time of reading, ending with a summary after completing their homework. After a week the diary is brought into the tutor period. In his introduction the tutor focuses pupils' attention on:

1 the part played by feelings in determining the approach to reading;
2 specifying problems;
3 setting targets for improvement.

The tutor will have to encourage pupils to observe themselves. Reminders, without nagging, seem to be necessary because pupils are liable to put off a new task. Those who fail to do it can, however, still benefit from the points made by others.

Study skills programmes give insufficient attention to feelings. When we paint a picture we take our total experience and personality to the task. This is seen very clearly in the art of the maladjusted pupil. Reading is not an exception to this. Many O-Level candidates have a pervasive sense of not being quite in control of their learning, indeed of their destinies. Ubiquity does not imply easy detection. The powerlessness is masked by hard work, conformity or an eager manner. This feeling is not intense enough to bring a prediction of failure, but it seems to contribute to underfunctioning. Failure to provide sufficient discussion of feelings related to study reinforces the negative influences of the peer group. Fifth year pupils can be in the position of an ambitious worker joining a work group whose norms are anti-work. The price of acceptance is abandoning overt expression of the desire to do well.

Anxiety about the ability to extract key elements, or the feeling that one is being perpetually criticized, reduces efficiency. Rigidity created by the search for *the* right answer, and failure to understand there are many ways of tackling a text, reduce independence.

Tutors must explore such issues through discussion. This is not a waste of time, for feelings have to be expressed if barriers to learning are to be removed. The middle range of ability and those slightly above this benefit most from such discussion, because the marginality of their position creates threat. O'Shea (1980), in her study of the Irish Leaving Certificate, found that middle ability pupils recorded the highest level of anxiety. Consolidation of positions into what Youngman (1978) has called 'disenchanted pupils' is another problem to be dealt with. He also detected a group whom he described as 'the worried'. These two types each formed 12 per cent of the first year intake, but it is likely they increase over the first four years of secondary schooling. One point of intervention is at the beginning of the fifth year when a key task is in sight. However, realism also requires us to recognize that some pupils will be untouched by this approach.

Treating skills in isolation without considering attitudes and feelings is sterile. Pupils' needs for autonomy and affiliation have to be considered. We need to help pupils construct their own model of effective reading, but we can help them to see the importance of examining the ways in which they distinguish between facts and opinions, statements and interpretations, the relevant and irrelevant. The underlying principle is that of encouraging pupils to take charge of their own learning.

MEMORY AND REVISION

Facts cannot be applied unless they are known. The desire to emphasize the skills of reasoning and of applying facts can obscure the need to improve memory. Pupils have difficulty in memorizing salient dates and names or cannot recall definitions and formulae. This leads to a haunting sense of inadequacy in some pupils. The aim is to induce recall of significant information. Learning and memory obviously go hand in hand, for what is understood is likely to be remembered. Yet even the undergraduate needs memory props.

If pupils have distinguished the salient points, they they can be organized through mnemonics. If possible, the mnemonic should include humour or personal associations. Examples are given in Table 17.

Table 17   Mnemonics.

English Literature
Pupils are often confused about who belongs to which family, therefore:
   My Romeo Cried Juliet
   reminds them that *Romeo* is a *Montague*
   and *Juliet* is a *Capulet*.

Biology
   a Annie builds   *Anabolism* is a process of building complex
      Cathy breaks   molecules from simple raw materials.
                      Catabolism is the process in which complex
                      substances are broken down into simpler
                      forms.

Table 17 – continued

b The vertebrae of the skeleton are difficult to remember.
The first two cervical vertebrae have specific names, and then
there are four types of vertebrae.
Agile Annie Catches The Long Snake
Atlas, Axis, Cervical, Thoracic, Lumbar, Sacral.

Chemistry
ALLOTROPES
*Desperately Forlorn Old Sinners Endlessly Ambling Through
Eternity Instinctively Send Prayers Somewhere.*
Different Forms Of Same Element Able To Exist In Same Physical
State.

Geography
Pupils often are confused by their inability to distinguish between:
The folds of an anticline   A
The folds of a syncline   V
Annie pointed up at Cynthia coming down.

Mathematics
a Polygons – naming in order of sides:

Triangle	*The*
Quadrilateral	*Quiet*
Pentagon	*Princess*
Hexagon	*Had*
Septagon	*Some*
Octagon	*Odd*
Nonagon	*New*
Decagon	*Drawers*

b Computer studies – software for translating computer
languages.
All Lovers Can Hate or ALCH!
Assembler translates a Low level language and a Computer
translates a High level language.

Such use of mnemonics is to be kept to a minimum. They are
more effective when incorporated into other methods. I have
found it useful to link mnemonics with the idea of 'thinking in
headlines' when working with examination candidates. Using
headlines provides the basis for organization. They form a
framework, allowing the pupil to subsume relevant facts under
each headline. The key word in each headline can be memorized
by building it into the mnemonic. Headlines are not to be confused with the trivial or dramatic; they are superordinate ideas
determining what is subsumed under them.

Diagrams allow one to use the headline approach to make obvious the logical structure of a topic, e.g.:

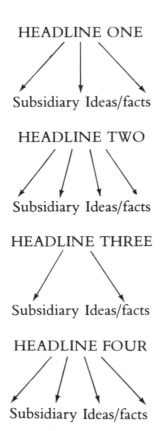

HEADLINE ONE

Subsidiary Ideas/facts

HEADLINE TWO

Subsidiary Ideas/facts

HEADLINE THREE

Subsidiary Ideas/facts

HEADLINE FOUR

Subsidiary Ideas/facts

Memorization during the revision period of the fifth year is a source of stress because pupils take an 'ingurgitating' position for far too long in homework periods. They do not test themselves frequently enough or check actively for errors and omissions. Variants of the strategy of revision laid out below have proved useful with both individuals and groups in fifth year revision.

1　Write down what you can recall about the topic to be revised.
2　Check what you have remembered for accuracy.
3　Skim through the section of your notebook covering the topic, noting any key points or headlines.
4　Read carefully for 12–18 minutes, making notes based on key points as you read.
5　Test yourself by a diagram or traditional notes. Some pupils find the tape recorder useful as a means of checking.

6 Repeat steps 4 and 5 until either the time you have allocated is almost exhausted or the topic has been reviewed.

7 Test your knowledge of the whole topic, checking carefully.

The tutor will have to train his form in this technique, allowing them to appreciate the benefits. It does not happen suddenly! Many pupils comment: 'I didn't think the time could go so quickly'; 'I feel on top of the work for the first time'; 'I am remembering a lot more. I didn't know it was possible to remember so much'.

ANXIETY AND REVISION

Anxiety is discussed elsewhere; so here the argument will focus on other aspects. We fail to make full use of pupils' emotional reaction to mock examinations. Yet these are very real, replicating later reactions at the June examinations. Pupils report:

1 a sense of separation and isolation from others, which they are unable to communicate to their parents or teachers.

2 the rise of panic with which they seem to have no means of coping.

3 the feeling of being powerless, often expressed in the initial complaint that they have no thoughts of their own.

4 the loss of the sense of planning and using time sensibly.

5 the realization that they lack guides for the selection of what is relevant and rejection of the irrelevant.

Susceptibility to such reactions obviously varies greatly between pupils both in type and intensity. Yet experience suggests that we can arouse such reactions without offering pupils the opportunity of examining and overcoming them. Under the pressure of the 'mocks' pupils are ready to examine their learning strategies even when they habitually rely on external direction. As one pupil put it, 'Surely there must be a better way than trying to learn it all off by heart!'

Post-mock examination defences can consist of lowering aspiration to a level where there is no sense of challenge. 'As long as I get C's I shan't mind. I will have got through' is a typical statement of those in this frame of mind. Ritual retreat, in which the motions of effort are made without real investment of self, is another defence. Time is then occupied, parents receiving the impression of conscientious preparation, but the processing and assimilation of material is minimal. Routine has become a defence against learning and a means of avoiding reality. Parents and teachers are then surprised at the poor results. Others use the 'insurance policy' strategy to anticipate their results by telling others how badly they expect to do.

Pupils should explore their feelings on entering the examination room, the strategies they used in tackling the questions and their ability to time themselves. Some have learned that it is a good idea to begin with one's best question as a confidence booster, only to dissipate any advantage by spending too much time on it. It is worth considering how pupils got ready the night before, and especially how they felt about the way in which they had prepared for the examinations. Realization of inadequacies often come at this moment, but is submerged by concern with marks. The tutor can reinstate those feelings soon after the examinations are completed and help pupils use them. The argument is therefore that the tutor must pay attention to the affective aspects of the 'mocks', and that this is as vital as the cognitive aspects which are the concern of the subject teacher.

Pupils need to discuss these feelings and reactions in a climate of acceptance. Initial discussion can be followed by a short look at learning beliefs, particularly those concerned with the locus of causality as described by Rotter (1966), Rotter *et al.* (1972) and Phares *et al.* (1976). We should, however, be clear that this is not a test. It is a way of stimulating discussion and producing awareness of issues. It takes this form:

Activity 59

BELIEFS ABOUT ACADEMIC SUCCESS

	Agree	Disagree	Uncertain	Comments
1 Sensible planning is a key factor in examination sucess.	.....	.....	.....	....
2 Pupils who do well in examinations usually get a lot of help from their parents.	.....	.....	.....	....
3 Teachers only praise you to make you work harder.	.....	.....	.....	....
4 When you fail it is usually because you did not work hard enough.	.....	.....	.....	....

5 A regular study
pattern usually   . . . .
leads to good   . . . .
results.   . . . .

6 I shall want to see
how I get on in my
O-Levels before I   . . . .
plan what to do   . . . .
next.   . . . .

7 When I get things
wrong it is because   . . . .
the teacher did not   . . . .
explain it clearly.   . . . .

8 If you are told you
don't have the   . . . .
ability there is no   . . . .
point in trying.   . . . .

9 Doing well in exams   . . . .
seems to be largely   . . . .
a matter of luck.   . . . .

10 At my age it is difficult   . . . .
to study because you   . . . .
have to go out with   . . . .
friends.   . . . .

11 I usually seem to do   . . . .
badly when I have to   . . . .
compete with others.   . . . .

12 People usually say the
exam was unfair when   . . . .
they haven't prepared   . . . .
for it.   . . . .

13 There is not much
point in trying to do
well if you are not
sure if you can get a   . . . .
good job when you   . . . .
leave school.   . . . .

14 Progress in a subject
depends on whether or   . . . .
not you like the   . . . .
teacher.   . . . .

15 You can learn how to   . . . .
do better next time   . . . .
from your mistakes.   . . . .

16 It seems to me that
who you know is more

important than your			. . . .
ability for success			. . . .
in life.	. . . . .	. . . . .	. . . . .	. . . .

17 Poor examination
results usually mean
that the candidate was
not taught properly.

18 When you do badly in
an essay it often
means that someone
was distracting you
in the lesson.

			. . . .
			. . . .
. . . . .	. . . . .	. . . . . .	. . . .
			. . . .
			. . . .
. . . . .	. . . . .	. . . . .	. . . .

On completion, discussion of the significance of the results takes place in small groups. The tutor begins by reminding the class of the tendency to attribute blame to others, and the need to accept responsibility for one's learning. Enough material for three or four tutorial periods should emerge from this questionnaire. If they are completed anonymously, the tutor can collect them and analyse the results, presenting them to the form. The aim is to examine the defensive responses to challenge and encourage a mature response to evaluation and stress. Beliefs about the nature of success are more influential in determining study plans than many pupils realize.

Mock examinations should alert pupils to areas of weakness while there is still time to effect corrective procedures. One can question whether this happens in the areas of study habits and the less content orientated aspects of preparation. The following questionnaire stimulated evaluation of the procedures used by students in preparing for the 'mocks'.

Activity 60

Evaluating Your Performance in the Mock Examinations

Why should you look at your mocks in this way?
Sometimes we concentrate too much on our marks, ignoring other important aspects of preparation for mock examinations. Feelings which influence our success are stirred up, and then subside to be forgotten until the real examinations are close. It is then too late to deal with them. We are aware of our strengths and weaknesses at the time of the mocks, yet we do little about them. The person who wants to be in control rather than feeling a victim does something about these things.

You may find it useful to answer these questions:

1 When you were revising for the mocks, how did you set about it?
   Some people have definite plans while others approach it
   blindly. Say what you did:

   . . . .
   . . . .

2 How satisfied were you with what you did? In what ways would
   you change the way you worked if you could begin preparing for
   the mocks again?

   . . . .
   . . . .
   . . . .

3 Briefly describe the way in which you tackled the examination
   papers, e.g. timing, order of questions, selection of questions,
   planning answers. If you feel you could improve your strategy,
   give details:

   . . . .
   . . . .
   . . . .

4 It is natural to feel anxious about examinations. The important
   thing is to use this anxiety to boost performance. How did you
   react to feeling anxious, depressed or uncertain when you
   revised? Could you be more constructive? If so, in what ways?

   . . . .
   . . . .
   . . . .

5 In some schools friends have grouped together to study and
   revise together. If you were to do this, how would you help one
   another?

   . . . .
   . . . .
   . . . .

The tutor could spend some time building the self-help groups.
Experienced teachers taking a B.Ed. course have found this valuable, while, amongst others, pupils living under conditions of
environmental stress and danger and Oxbridge candidates have
both reported favourably on it. We complain about the negative
influence of the peer group, yet it can be a source of help in
achieving educational aims when used in this way. First year sixth
form students can be brought in to give advice and help to the fifth
year once such approaches are under way in the school.

Confidence is the antithesis of anxiety. It is therefore imperative
that we explore ways in which confidence can be developed as a

counter-measure to anxiety. In what ways can the pupils create a realistic sense of confidence? When pupils are encouraged to look at this topic they see that confidence is related to the sense of being in control of one's learning and the development of self-management. It may be tempting to attack the false confidence which hides inner doubt. But it *is* a defence, and to attack it blindly is to increase doubt, and thus be destructive. Private intervention by tutor or head of year is essential. In public we should concentrate on the positive otherwise pupils resist tutorial work because of the danger of losing face.

Confidence is enhanced by simple measures aimed at building a sense of competence. Pupils can be encouraged to use the concept of 'anchoring ideas': these are two or three ideas associated with a topic which form the structure for notes or a diagram. The 'anchoring ideas' are written in a bright colour, giving them salience. They act as cues to the pupil which reinstate what has been associated with them. This psychological significance seems to be that for many pupils they structure the learning task and make it manageable.

In building up an individually satisfying revision system the tutor should remind pupils of the discussion on self-management and the timing of activities. If this has not been done, it is imperative that he deals with the issue. Ausubel (1968) shows that relatively little attention has been given to the relation between frequency of revision and the retention of meaningful facts. The question of distributed revision or when it is most effective has to be considered too. Crudely put, there are two apparently opposite strategies. Revision can occur shortly after the material has been tackled and it is relatively fresh in the learner's mind, or after a period during which a considerable amount has been forgotten. The first seems to be the most sensible, but this is not necessarily so.

Early work in study skills showed that fifth and sixth form pupils did not use the teacher's comments on their work; therefore they were less aware than they could have been of their weaknesses and what they needed to learn. The target of effort should be that which has not been retained. It is evident that this is the material which has not acquired significance for the learner. With longer intervals the poorly assimilated or ill-understood material becomes more evident, and the learner, *if trained*, pays special attention to it. Quick revision appears to increase consolidation of knowledge largely because the learner is still sensitive to the struc-

ture and significance of what he has learned. Revision after a
longer interval leads to an awareness of what has not been well
learned and therefore forgotten.

A combination of immediate and delayed revision seems to be
indicated, provided we see that frequency of review is only of
limited value. Active striving by the learner to understand and
translate the ideas into his own terms is essential. This is fostered
by training in the formulation and insertion of questions and answers into their notes. They can be put in by coloured pen to
distinguish them from the original material. A simple training
exercise often takes this form:

1　Students look through the material to be revised.
2　They underline key phrases.
3　Key phrases associated with what they consider to be likely to
　present difficulty are boxed in with a bright colour.
4　Consolidation is attempted through a diagram.
5　Students formulate a question about the material, taking the
　standpoint of the teacher.
6　They then produce an answer to their question, ending by
　checking its accuracy.

The tutor will remind students of the need to search for key
points and signposts in the text, coupled with the injunction to pay
special attention to any instructions or limitations set out in the
teacher's handouts or students' notes on the lesson.

It would be delightful if one could give a universal recipe for
success but there is no right way of learning. The position is
complicated because the connections between controlled
laboratory-type experiments and the life of the classroom are
unclear. Ausubel (1968) argues that distributed practice is more
effective than massed practice for both learning and retention,
with qualifications. Personality, age, social background, intelligence and motivation affect the response to revision strategies. Distributed revisions may be more productive for the younger and
less able pupil. We have known for years the impact of birth date
and consequent entry to school on pupils' performances. Wide
ranges of attitudes and levels of maturity in the fifth year demand
adaptation rather than uniformity. The greater the motivation and
ability of the adolescent to invest significance and meaning in his
subjects, the less important is distributed learning. With a student
who has the motivation and ability, the massed effort is probably
more rewarding. We cannot advocate conformity to a single
approach: some students will need spaced practices, but others

may find that the intensive activity of massed practice is their best way. Experience of both should be encouraged and the student encouraged to select what he feels to be right for him.

Again, a warning is necessary. There are the occasional students who rely almost totally upon association. Their approach has the appearance of sequential learning, yet it lacks the logic of this as the bonds between the elements are idiosyncratic. These students need to be approached cautiously. Clumsy intervention produces disorganization in them. The skill of outlining in which they look at salient arguments, pay attention to the ordering of elements and reach a general conclusion can be helpful if they are taught to do it slowly and patiently in individual sessions; public intervention is likely to produce resentment or feelings of inferiority.

Two further points should be made. First, it is obviously profit- . able for the tutor to have had his group in the fourth year. He is then aware of possible reactions and has identified those who are at risk. Second, application of a simple rule-of-thumb approach called the 20/80 rule will guide our efforts. We cannot deal with everything, and the rule points out that 20 per cent of pupils will account for 80 per cent of the problems of study encountered. Of the problems exhibited, about 20 per cent will be the focal ones on which the tutor should expend 80 per cent of the time he invests in helping these pupils. This guide is clearly simplistic, but it is surprising how it aids the tutor.

ANXIETY AND COPING WITH TENSION

Spielberger *et al.* (1976) point out that reducing test anxiety is insufficient to increase academic performance. Defective study skills have to be remedied. In examining tensions we should be aware that the pupils in the middle range of ability may experience more tension and anxiety. The goals are meaningful and desired, although self-comparison with the brighter pupils coupled with the comments of teachers produce uncertainty and self-doubt. Anxiety can act as an energizer, but for the middle ability group who occupy a marginal position in achievement of academic success it can be debilitating. Ability is a relevant variable which the tutor has to take into account. A study by Spielberger and Weitz (1964) found that high anxiety facilitated the performance of students at the highest level of ability, but had detrimental effects on others.

Test anxiety diverts attention away from the task, as Mandler and Sarason (1952) suggest. Attention is directed by the test-anxious student to his feelings, his behaviour and the reactions of others rather than the demands of the task. Self-orientated and task-irrelevant reactions undoubtedly reduce efficiency in examinations. Students have self-definitions which include such things as, 'I am one of those who just can't cope with examinations', 'I always get into a panic the night before and then can't do anything in the exam', or 'My mind always goes blank when I try to answer a question'. Some help can be derived from exploration of these questions, although severe cases may need help from the educational psychologist.

Our use of mock examinations may be less productive than it should be. Do we really explore pupils' reactions in ways which allow them to master self-diminishing experiences? Feelings and behaviours become evident at the 'mocks' but are allowed to subside only to be resurrected in the real examinations in an unmodified way. Students report:

1 a sense of separation from others, and that key figures in their lives do not understand how they are feeling.
2 the rise of a sense of panic.
3 feelings of having no thoughts of their own.
4 moving into a state where they do not care about what happens: this is not real indifference, but something close to depression.
5 loss of the sense of timing and planning.
6 awareness that they are including irrelevant material in their revision and answers accompanied by an apparent inability to do anything about it.

The strength and number of such reactions vary between individuals. It is not sufficient to say they must learn to cope with them as part of life, for they reduce performance and lessen the impact of good teaching. If left unexplored, they may cause some pupils to perceive their teachers as dominating and pressurizing rather than as providing assistance and understanding. A surprising number see their teachers as using examinations to instil fear and obedience. Perhaps we over-rely on pupils' confidence in their teachers. Confidence in the teacher's ability does not reduce examination anxiety even in that teacher's subject area. Perception of teacher competence is an independent issue, although perceived teacher incompetence obviously reinforces anxiety.

A sense of helplessness and disorganization are the key factors. This is reduced by the tutors dealing with the practical elements of planning as well as with feelings. Balance sheets which allow students to evaluate the strengths as well as the weaknesses of the performance bring back a sense of control. This is then reinforced by planning realistic targets for improvement and the development of self-help groups in which pupils work together, planning their strategies. The constructive use of the Easter vacation is an important element in this planning: a balanced investment of time during the vacation allows pupils to approach the final period of preparation more confidently.

The tutor will find it helpful to look at the function of predictions in shaping pre-examination strategies, the role of the comparison process in strengthening a feeling of inferiority, and the tendency to procrastinate. We have a responsibiilty to teach pupils about the processes which impinge on their performance. This can be done quite simply by attractively presented material which gets to the main elements of learning processes. The samples below (Figs 18–21) may stimulate tutors and heads of year to produce their own.

What appears to be negative can be used positively. Any crisis contains within it the seeds of growth. The comparison process provides an example. Usually it reinforces the sense of failure, as students weigh themselves against others and find themselves wanting. The positive approach is to ask the learner to find several people doing well in the area of deficiency, get to know them, finding out how they tackle the subject. They do not emulate these people blindly, but select what they find useful, building on it in a way which suits them. The others function not just as models, but as 'benchmarks' against which the anxious or inadequate student can compare his progress.

The tutor will call students' attention to the need to analyse experiences. What they see as general examination anxiety may turn out to be specific anxiety stemming from one or two subjects. This can be taken further. Anxiety about English may be anxiety about certain components – spelling, speed and legibility of writing – or the feeling that it is difficult to say exactly what one means. With mathematics, anxiety may not be about the whole subject: it may be conditioned anxiety associated with arithmetical computation, predictions of inability to find the right approach to problems, or difficulty in working quickly enough. The tutor alerts students to the need to look more closely at what they call anxiety, making sense out of what was amorphous. He should then urge students to make full use of the subject specialist. After-

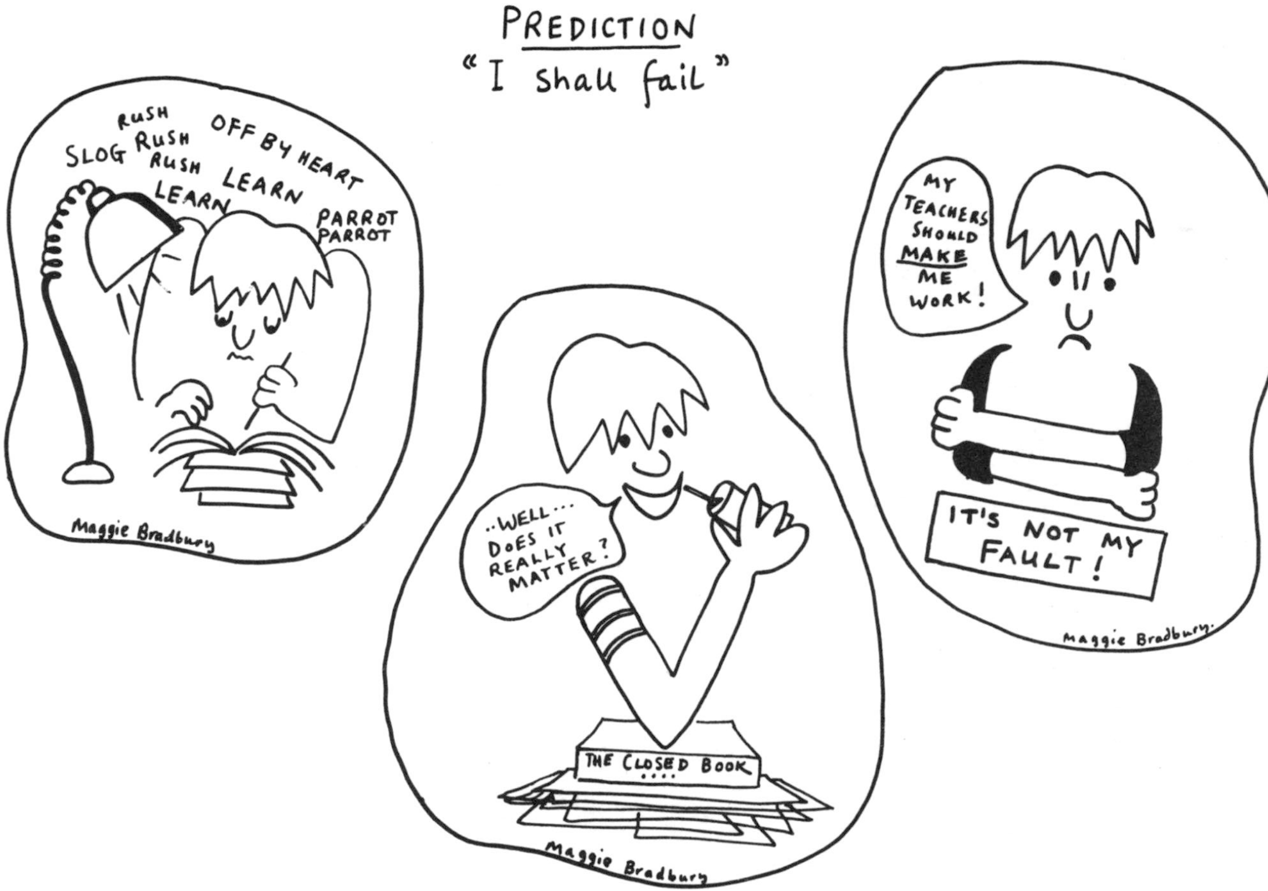
PREDICTION
"I shall fail"
RUSH
SLOG RUSH
RUSH
OFF BY HEART
LEARN
LEARN
PARROT
PARROT
Maggie Bradbury
..WELL... DOES IT REALLY MATTER?
THE CLOSED BOOK ....
Maggie Bradbury
MY TEACHERS SHOULD MAKE ME WORK!
IT'S NOT MY FAULT!
Maggie Bradbury.

Figure 18

Well, you are beginning to think.
BUT what about your ATTITUDES
and your MOTIVATION. After all,
why are you in the Sixth Form?

ATTITUDES:

1. These boil down to ⟶ Being a pawn.

↘ Taking full
responsibility
for your success.

2. WHAT DO WE KNOW ABOUT FAILURES?

The answer is, "Quite a lot!" The failures are:-

PAWNS WHO ⟶ Believe in luck
and chance as
important factors
in life.
Blame other people-
teachers, parents,
friends, when they
don't do well.
Give up easily and
allow themselves to
be put off.
Accept that they
can't do it and
that they haven't
the ability.

Figure 19

Now what about the successes?

Well, what do you expect?

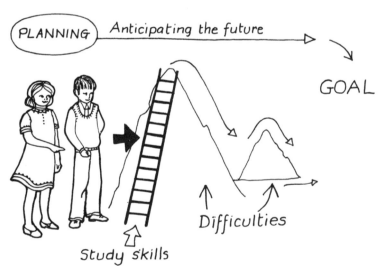

SUCCESSES — TAKE RESPONSIBILITY FOR THEMSELVES

When they meet difficulties or frustration they say, "WHAT AM I DOING THAT NEEDS TO BE CHANGED?" So they look at their study skills and revise them. They seek help in an intelligent way. They PLAN AHEAD and anticipate the future.

PLANNING — Anticipating the future

GOAL

Difficulties

Study skills

Figure 20

school 'mathematics clinics' have proved very useful in one school as a way of examining these problems.

Post-'mock' defences need to be examined. Some students respond to mocks by the 'insurance policy' approach in which

NEXT :

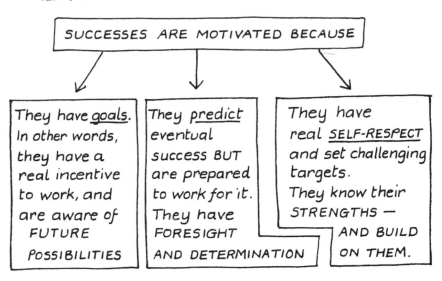

SUCCESSES ARE MOTIVATED BECAUSE

They have goals. In other words, they have a real incentive to work, and are aware of FUTURE POSSIBILITIES

They predict eventual success BUT are prepared to work for it. They have FORESIGHT AND DETERMINATION

They have real SELF-RESPECT and set challenging targets. They know their STRENGTHS — AND BUILD ON THEM.

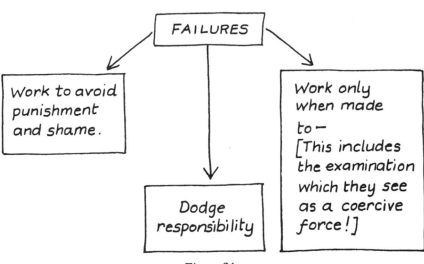

FAILURES

Work to avoid punishment and shame.

Dodge responsibility

Work only when made to — [This includes the examination which they see as a coercive force!]

Figure 21

they broadcast expectations of doing badly. This mechanism, intended to cover its user against the possibility of poor results, can create a self-fulfilling prophecy. Some retreat to a routine performance which involves little active planning, while others lower their level of aspiration unnecessarily.

Simple activities help:

Activity 61

The following comments are written on the blackboard under the heading *Examination Strategies*:

    1 Research shows that when students make a mistake early in an examination they are more error-prone later in that examination and tend to misinterpret questions.

    2 Many students write good answers, but to different questions from those set.

    3 A surprising number of students run out of time, and are unable to tackle the last question or leave it uncompleted.

    4 Papers often contain obvious mistakes which have not been crossed out.

Students then discuss the relevance of these statements to their own method of tackling the examination, incorporating it into a diagram.

Mandler and Sarason (1952) show that the cognitive element in test anxiety is self-instruction which is failure inducing: 'I will get into a panic and then there is no point in continuing'. This can be used constructively. An example is given below of the way in which students can verbalize new ways of coping.

Activity 62

After the tutor has discussed briefly the way in which students can define themselves, as failures or as those who cannot cope with examinations, they are given the following worksheet:

Learning to Improve Performance

1 Choose a source of difficulty in revision, answering questions, or in examinations, and discuss it with a friend.
Write down in this box exactly what goes wrong or creates difficulty.

```
┌─────────────────────────────────────────────────┐
│                                                   │
│                                                   │
│                                                   │
│                                                   │
│                                                   │
└─────────────────────────────────────────────────┘
```

2 As we come into a situation we start thinking about it, predicting how we will behave, e.g. 'I will make a good start, get so far, and

then find I can't do it'. Write down in the next box what usually comes into your mind.

```
┌─────────────────────────────────────────────────────────┐
│                                                         │
│                                                         │
│                                                         │
│                                                         │
│                                                         │
└─────────────────────────────────────────────────────────┘
```

3 Now work out with your friend the steps you could take to improve the situation. Put them into step-by-step instructions as if you were teaching someone else how to behave sensibly in the situation. Write your instructions below:

```
┌─────────────────────────────────────────────────────────┐
│                                                         │
│                                                         │
│                                                         │
│                                                         │
│                                                         │
└─────────────────────────────────────────────────────────┘
```

4 Now repeat them to your friend. You can then, if you really wish to change, use these instructions to master the situation which causes the difficulty.

```
┌─────────────────────────────────────────────────────────┐
│                                                         │
│                                                         │
│                                                         │
│                                                         │
└─────────────────────────────────────────────────────────┘
```

The reader may feel that undue attention has been given to examination anxiety, and that this reflects a limited view of education. But this book is concerned with a limited topic, study skills, and examinations are of great concern to pupils and parents. To ignore anxiety, doubts about competence and the processes through which pupils learn is the equivalent of passing by on the other side.

THE MANAGEMENT OF TENSIONS

Tension permeates the fifth year. Doubts about the future compound present anxieties in the field of study. In this complex situation we can put some of the facts at the disposal of students, encouraging them to explore the ways in which they manage tensions. Stress produces the temptation to take the path of expediency which yields immediate relief and allows the individual to escape from the sense of coercion.

Fight or flight are the basic tendencies around which modes of tension reduction occur. Each solution will cost something, although there is no way of estimating these costs without knowledge of the individual and his background. We have already seen that some individuals tend to see themselves as pawns or passive reactors to forces beyond their control. Tendencies to reject responsibility for oneself become operative under prolonged stress. The answer in our role of tutor responsible for a group of pupils is not to try to change the source of stress, even if we disapprove of it, but to equip the student to react less adversely. Maladaptive resolution of tension includes the use of denial mechanisms, perseverance of rigid or inappropriate responses, regression to earlier over-dependency upon teacher direction, the attribution of negative intent to teachers, re-evaluation of the importance of achievement, and displacing aggression into conflicts with peers or siblings. This catalogue should be sufficient to explain why such topics have to be included in a programme of study skills. These patterns of behaviour are unlikely to be accompanied by effective study.

Fight and flight are difficult to disentangle, for both are ways of leaving the field of tension. Students who spend time in aggressively criticizing the school and devaluing teachers are still engaging in avoidance. Within the form they adopt the role of the 'resident cynic' who pours cold water on all that the tutor attempts. Denial is an attempt to insulate oneself against pressures, but it courts failure for the urgency of the situation is suppressed. Provocative role-taking involving brash assertions of independence, bravado and emphasis on the lack of relevance of school success to life are some examples of risky tension reduction.

Tutors can open up these ways of coping through discussion. The danger is that we slip into admonition or moralizing, postures which offer pupils an excuse to disregard the tutor. The presentation of cartoons can initiate discussion. The small groups then produce a set of cartoons which illustrate self-defeating modes of coping with tension. Simple exercises, where pupils are presented with situations and then select the most effective way of coping, also work, provided that the tutor ensures that the final section of the period applies the learning to the pupils' immediate situation.

Parents often become the target for aggression when the pupil is under stress. Reversion to maintenance of identity by blind opposition occurs when parents lack the capacity to understand, and then adapt to the stress of their children before examinations. In these circumstances, family tensions and partially resolved stresses become operative again. In a more sinister way, unresolved conflicts about parents' achievements in their adolescence shape interaction with the child. The resultant emotional blackmail, crude comparisons with other family members and a barrage of criticism erode the pupils' desire to work. Pupils are often more aware than their parents that the past is being re-enacted, but are powerless to deal with it.

Escalation of tensions is often accompanied by communication patterns within the family based on mutual mistrust and suspicion. Parents are seen as failing to offer support, retreating to 'Do what you think is best. All I want is for you to be happy', or engaging in destructive criticism which leave the child with the impression of insatiable parents whose expectations can never be met.

Identity is vulnerable in fifth year pupils. Parental expression of anxieties are interpreted in some cases as denial of individuality, and that boundaries are being breached, forcing the child back to earlier dependencies. At such moments the family may produce intolerable strains on its members (Cooper, 1977).

The direct approach is for the head of year and the tutor to organize discussion groups for parents, providing them with the opportunity to give vent to their frustrations and discuss methods of constructive support. Both are important. The tutor can spend some time on helping pupils cope more adequately with stressful incidents. These cluster around issues of:

1 Noise, the playing of music while studying.
2 Parental evaluations of the influence of friends.
3 Insistence by the mother on staying in the bedroom to study.
4 Inconsistencies in parental signals about the probability of success or failure. The pupil gets the contradictory messages, 'You are going to do well, but you are likely to fail'.
5 Resentment because the adolescent feels he is valued for his achievement rather than for himself. Acceptance is seen as conditional on performance.
6 Comparisons with relations and references to 'what people will think!'
7 Nagging – from the child's perspective.

Any tutor can take the issues and present them as situations to which students have to find answers. In evaluating the strategies or responses suggested the tutor should direct attention towards the short run and long term consequences of actions. Another key element will be the consideration of the sources of influence which help them come to a decision. Pupils delude themselves that they are making the decision, when it is often anticipation of the reactions of friends that is the main element in their solution. Simple activities simulate the desire to cope such as this questionnaire and idea for a tape. Note that we avoid implying that parental pressures are necessarily a problem.

Activity 63
Study Pressures
  1 List the things that *you* find difficult to cope with when studying at home for the examinations.
  2 In small groups of three or four, share ideas about the most sensible ways of dealing with these difficulties.
  3 Parents are very anxious to help their children in these matters. Are there any ways in which your parents could be of help? Discuss your approach in asking them. (Sometimes we can be aggressive about what we want or make the other person feel guilty!)

Activity 64
Tape: Family Misunderstanding
Mother: Jane, you have been watching television rather a long time: oughtn't you to go upstairs and get down to some study?
Jane: I've done quite a lot of work earlier today – you know how it is – you can get fed up. I feel I want a break.
Mother: But you were out with your friends again last night, and came in very late.
Jane: Mum, be fair! Life is just too short to keep on working endlessly. I have a right to enjoy myself.
Mother: Look, Jane, we've had this out before. You want a decent job – you don't want to end up on the dole like that girl Sue, wasn't it – that you used to go around with. Go up and get on with some work, please.
Jane: When I've finished watching this.
Mother: No, go now. I'm your mother!
Jane: The trouble with you is you always want your own way. You don't think I want any fun. Stop nagging!

Mother: I always said you were an ungrateful child – not like your sister Mary. She did well at college. Now, no more nonsense. Get upstairs at once!

Jane: Oh, get lost! You never stop nagging from first thing in the morning to last thing at night. I bet you nag when you talk in your sleep.

Mother: That's enough! Where's your father? (Calls) Bill, come quickly.

Father: What's going on? Now look here, my girl, when I was your age I had to earn my own living. Stop upsetting your mother and get up to your room. Just think what your mother and I have done for you – why aren't you grateful?

Jane: Stop keeping on at me! I don't want to do those so-and-so exams. I'm going down to Emma's and if I come back tonight you'll be lucky. You don't understand anything.

(Jane rushes out, slamming the door.)

Groups discuss:

1 The standpoint of parents and the girl.
2 Why they think the mother gets trapped into nagging.
3 Could she have shown her worry and concern more acceptably?
4 The effects of such situations on study.
5 What is the impact of statements about nagging or being grateful in such situations?

Peer groups influence achievement. At various points in this book suggestions have been made for ways in which friends can work together and self-help groups based on co-operation can be developed. Teachers express concern because the peer group seems to have a compulsive influence on performance. This is part of a wider process beyond the limited purpose of this book. Pastoral care is concerned with these processes and pupils can be given the skills of coping with the taunts of a friend who has invited them to play truant when the invitation is refused. In many ways we can give pupils the skills of refusing to adopt certain behaviours while still enjoying the friendship of a group. Pupils can learn that they do not have to indulge in all the behaviours found in a group because they find membership of it attractive. The group has no right to impose an identity on them.

Open discussion about the reactions when labelled as a 'creep', and the costs of passively adhering to a norm about the desired output of work, will be sufficient to alert some pupils to the dangers. But need we see peer groups in negative terms? Expectations of peers may be positive and the achieving pupil is often admired. Kandel and Lesser (1972) show that values of parents and children are very similar and that dependence on the peer group does not mean a decline in parental influence. The question that has to be answered is what needs does the peer group meet for its members. If we reduce threat, set out to use friends and stimulate co-operation through self-help groups, the peer group can raise the level of performance rather than restrict it.

Adolescents differ most from adults about the importance of immediate rewards as a source of satisfaction. Peer group support in small friendship groups can be a source of support to pupils as they strive towards important goals. The idea of life space diagrams (produced by Lewin, 1935) can be of great help. Pupils can work out hazards, obstacles, and sources of aid in a constructive way through such diagrams. They then proceed to plan the way in which they can help one another. The reader will find an excellent description of life space diagrams in Lazarus (1969).

This chapter intentionally avoids repeating material. The reader may well find some of the activities set out in earlier chapters of use if study skills have not been developed systematically in the first four years of the secondary school.

5: The Sixth Form

THE CONTEXT OF LEARNING

The sixth form student should be committed to thinking about his thinking and learning about his learning. The mechanics of study skills are best developed in earlier years, although Dean *et al.* (1978) and Jacobs (1974) found many sixth form students still experienced difficulty with note-taking. Over-reliance on teacher handouts, failure to make notes which clearly distinguish between the significant and the marginal, and dependence on memorization as a major technique is common. The result is superficial learning, and a sense of alienation from what is learned. Study is then contaminated by the sense that one is engaged in an impossible task.

By the time the sixth form is reached, the student's approach to learning has crystallized; awareness of deficiencies and of the desirability of change is insufficient to overcome the dislike or fear of change. This is one example of the pervasive ambivalence that has to be reckoned with in sixth form guidance. It would be false to claim that attitudes to achievement in the sixth form are necessarily positive and straightforward.

The context of learning has to be taken into account. Sixth form students are often in conflict – indeed, Williams (1979) has aptly described it as an arena. Divisiveness rather than unity, competition and provocation rather than co-operation and support, mark the student-created climate in which learning takes place. A sense of evaluation by peers, and vulnerability to their assessments, impinge upon performance.

Deep concern about acceptability causes many students to ruminate obsessively about relationships while enthusiastically working to destroy one. Competitiveness in personal relationships is paralleled by conflicts about intellectual endeavour. Ambivalence manifests itself in that some desire success and yet procrastinate. Endorsement of the desirability of intellectual achievement does not prevent avoidance of the effort involved in study.

Divisiveness takes many forms. Even where physical circumstances do not restrict contact, a divide exists between upper and
lower sixth. Valuable experiences and sources of influence are then
denied to the first year sixth. This system-based division is
accompanied by other divisions. Traditional sixth form students
regard the less academic ones with suspicion. In turn, the 'new'
sixth form reciprocate by a dislike which scarcely masks a sense of
inferiority. They then take up a defensive stance. Denial of these
things is an act of collusion by the tutor, who is led into supporting a false definition of reality. Those responsible for guidance in
the sixth form have to face these facts squarely.

Hazards and insecurity in relationships are hidden by reactions
which diminish attainment. Postures of indifference, toughness
and cynicism are struck which reduce effectiveness in the area of
learning. Once taken, they cannot be abandoned without loss of
face. But again the ambivalence manifests itself. Individuals still
desire that which they are ostensibly rejecting. Cynicism conceals
the desire to trust. Belief in the need for openness in relationships
is accompanied by the fear that one will be compelled to present a
false face; while achievement, if gained, is reduced to an outcome
produced by luck.

Ambivalence can occasionally reach the point where the student
no longer feels real. Feelings close to those of de-personalization
arise. Studying seems to be an automatic process in which the self
is not involved. Such students feel distant from the learning process. As teachers we can fail to see these things operating in the
sixth form. Perhaps we find it disconcerting to be asked to take
such factors into account at the moment when academic concerns
are at their strongest in the secondary school. We then retreat to the
position where we say, 'I am paid to teach'.

Sixth form membership is both voluntary and contractual.
Students have – to differing degrees – consciously defined themselves as those who can benefit from sixth form experience. But
this does not mean that identity as a learner is not problematical.
Students feel that they are required to function within a context of
learning, where the self of the learner is taken for granted or
defined in arbitrary terms, for example, as 'Oxbridge material'.
Doubts about the validity of learning are reinforced. People who
are at a stage of development which makes them value spontaneity
and honesty can interpret, perhaps misinterpret, the learning
required of them as the production of socially acceptable
responses.

The brief statement above condenses and sharpens the issues. The reader should be alerted to the emotional forces which blunt the capacity for learning. Yet they are not necessarily negative. Thinking and feeling enrich each other. In this stage of potential developmental tensions and ambivalences, the tutorial group can be of great significance. The tutor must bring intellect to bear on the task, using his subject specialization as a tool in developing understanding of conflicts in the field of achievement. He presents himself to students as a model of intellectual competence who also understands the doubts and insecurities inherent in striving for excellence. He does not make the error of equating achievement with competition. The efficient tutor will have discovered that the more we help students explore their underlying feelings, the greater is their capacity for applying their intellect with precision. With this age group, who overtly stress their independence, we may see how dependent they are on us to produce a better atmosphere for learning. Yet this has always been the strength of the good sixth form.

If the school has failed to induce the basic mechanics of study skills, then they have to be taught quickly. One answer is a two-day crash course, backed by periodic reviews and extensions on four occasions in the first term. The course would be focused on note-taking, the use of diagrams, effective reading and self-management. Students entering the sixth form must face the success eroding outcomes of attitudes behind these common statements:

'O-Levels are the worst thing than can happen to me.'

'What's all the fuss about? I know how to study. I passed my O-Levels, didn't I?'

'After all, there's plenty of time. I've got two years before I take my A-Levels.'

The material in Chapter Four will be useful in devising a crash course for sixth form entrants. It is imperative, however, that as soon as possible the tutor helps students examine their style of thinking and the deeper aspects of learning.

THE SIXTH FORM STUDENT'S STYLE OF LEARNING

Tutors with the sixth form student invite rejection if they attempt guidance without realizing the constraints stemming from the developmental problems of trust and openness. Many forces push students towards feeling inferior, creating the need for defences which stress a pseudo-independence and superiority. Expectations of friends and others, although positive, assume a compulsive character, and are a source of threat. Vulnerability to signals of derogation produces problems for the tutor which can only be understood when he understands that at some period in the sixth form career many students reach the point of doubting the legitimacy of their own wishes and positive expectations.

Underfunctioning in this age is related to the lack of essential skills of thinking, incapacity in studying constructively without direct supervision, emotional insecurity which creates susceptibility to negative forms of comparison and rigidity. The tutor has to be aware that rigidity takes many forms. Basically, it narrows perceptions and limits the range of learning behaviour. The rigid sixth form student typically claims that he is only in the sixth form 'to get good A-Levels'. Preoccupation with the outcome prevents him from assessing the validity of the means he is employing. Rigidity is accompanied by resistance to change, concrete thinking, and striving to do the acceptable thing in a somewhat compulsive way. This seems to be accompanied by limited strategies of learning, over-reliance upon memorization being the most common. The rigid pupil seems unable to modify his original orientation despite evidence that it is unproductive.

Combination of the demands of the transition, and the feeling of success in arriving here, create a climate in which the tutor can explore rigidity and its accompanying superficial learning with his group. By the second term it would be too late: ennui and habitual responses will have reasserted themselves.

Subjects for exploration in tutor groups in the first term:
The basic skill which has to be developed is that of inferential thinking. On this we base the ability to assess the quality of the evidence. Students have to be trained to think more flexibly about the data. Not only must they question its validity and sufficiency but they must ask what is the degree of likelihood that their inference is true or false. The concepts of probability and reasonable doubt or certainty in drawing inferences should be introduced early in the guidance sessions.

The aim of these sessions is to help students to see that the style of thought demanded of them is basically scientific, even if they are studying arts subjects. All have to think in terms of the evidence and hypotheses, testing the latter by the available facts, and by rational argument. Part of our aim here is to help students appreciate that the truth which is the object of intellectual endeavour is conditional, propositional and relative rather than absolute. Awareness that the interpretation of facts, and the view of truth that predominates is an emergent product of a particular epoch is no mean tool for further intellectual development.

We might then move to looking at pupils' beliefs about causality. Hume pointed out long ago that because things occur in a regular sequence we may assume causality where there is merely contiguity. This is germane to the treatment of evidence. Students shift from recognition of a relationship of association to the attribution of causality without questioning the legitimacy of the assumption. In working with this age group I have found it useful to begin exploring the topic by looking at 'Why things happen to us'. The discussion then centres on the key question, 'Do we have certain organized systems of expectations which determine what happens to us?' The objective is to alert students to the fact that our perceptions of causality may be crucial in determining our success and mode of functioning in the world. We have already seen in an earlier chapter, the importance of the tendency to attribute causation to oneself or to the environment.

Students find it helpful to discuss readiness to attribute causation, and are impressed by the need to be aware of it. Michotte (1954) demonstrated the far-reaching nature of the tendency. Rectangles were shown moving towards or away from one another under varying speeds, distance and direction. The viewers often saw one rectangle as the cause of the movement of another, although they actually did not make contact. Variation in the type of movement also had an influence on the attribution: jerky movement was associated with mechanical causation; smooth, undulating movement was related to living creatures. Equally important were the differences in readiness to attribute purpose in this way. Some students did, but others did not. Unfortunately, we have little knowledge of the personality factors which underlie the difference.

Heider and Simmel (1944) also looked at the topic. When individuals were shown two triangles – one larger than the other – and a disc moving around amongst rectangles, animism accompanied causality. Reports of the movement witnessed were couched in terms of fighting, chasing, attacking and evading. But the viewers referred to family situations, conflict between parents and child. While the large triangle was described as bullying, aggressive and mean, the smaller triangle was seen as heroic and defiant. Evidence of this type leads one into fuller discussion of the students' habitual ways of assuming causality.

The tutor provides simple examples for discussion – the tendency to attribute the behaviour of others to personality traits and character (e.g. he is an aggressive person), but one's own behaviour to the situation – 'What else could I do?' Examination of this topic is crucial. We are reminded that we are, at least partially, responsible for the environmental stresses and responses of which we complain. Furthermore, some of this age group retain below their surface activities a maladaptive state of learned helplessness, believing that skills will not alleviate their plight. Their theme is, 'There is nothing I can do about it.' Resistance to study skills is sometimes based on such beliefs. Entry to the sixth form and its new demands can reinforce this orientation to life and learning.

We may now return to inferential thinking. Basically this relates to the student's evaluation of the data, and the use he makes of it. Students can be given a passage with a number of conclusions which apparently derive from it. They are then asked if they consider them to be valid. Discussion then moves to the degree of risk which lies in drawing inferences. From this, the emphasis moves to detection of assumptions. All too often, impressive statements or arguments are based on very doubtful assumptions which go unchallenged. We have to train all our sixth form students to incorporate the following questions into their thinking.

1 What is the speaker/writer taking for granted? Is he justified in this?
2 Is the argument biased?
3 Does his conclusion follow from the evidence he has given?
4 Have I gone beyond the evidence?

Sixth form students enjoy constructing counter-arguments – perhaps a remnant of the adolescent tendency to gain identity by opposition – testing their own construction against the original one. It also seems helpful to encourage them to examine the implications of a particular viewpoint, beginning by asking, 'What is he protesting about or arguing against?'

Our next step in the study skills programme is to begin examining the ways in which students tackle problems in their subjects. Initial discussion might centre on the question, 'Do we scan the total situation or do we tend to pay attention only to a few points which we assume to be important?' Levelling and sharpening are well researched areas in cognition. Bartlett's (1932) work on social factors in recall and Allport and Postman's (1945) investigation of the psychology of rumour are still helpful in considering problem solving. Extreme types are met infrequently, but students need to be aware that they may have an unrecognized preference for either levelling or sharpening, which affects their problem-solving ability. The tendency of the sharpener to centre on a few points that possess significance for him reduces the range of scanning and distorts perception of the problem. Centration reduces the range of examination of the material, and leads to distortion and over-simplification. Treating everything as of equal importance brings difficulties of organization and attack.

Closely associated with this preference for levelling or sharpening is the ability to adjust to new information in learning. Byrne (1964) discusses repression versus sensitization as an element in perception and judgement. In many ways this appears to be linked to scanning behaviour. The repressors look less at the total situation, while sensitizors scan it more thoroughly. Repressors are less likely to discriminate adequately. The point of this material is to show tutors the need to stimulate students to reflect on their learning style rather than approach it blindly. Levellers will deny differences or prefer to ignore them, whereas sharpeners enjoy making discriminations. Again, there is the possibility that those who tend to level may be tied to their original perceptions of the problem, and do not adjust to new evidence or accept that their original definition of the situation was incomplete.

The most constructive way of building awareness of conceptual style may be to present students with a series of problems culled from various sources. A well-known example is provided below.

Activity 65
A problem
You are in Africa in the last century at a time when missionary activity was most intense. Three missionaries and three cannibals who are potential converts have arrived at the bank of a wide, crocodile-ridden river. Your task is to plan how to get them across the river safely. There is a rowing boat which will hold two people, i.e. the rower and a passenger. All the missionaries can row, but only one of the cannibals has this ability — their contact with the joys of civilization have been brief. Thus the complication is that under no circumstances must the cannibals outnumber the missionaries on either bank at any time. The reasons for this are obvious. Check your answer: it is quite

*possible to fool yourself, and not see that at some stage in the operation
you have not met the basic condition.*

After three minutes, partner work is allowed. The tutor raises
questions after the time he allows has elapsed. They may take
the following form:

1 How do you habitually approach problems?
2 Do you have some principle for deciding what are the
   important elements of a problem?
3 How do you decide what is relevant and what is im-
   material?
4 Do you search actively for factors which might change the
   situation and lead to a solution?
5 Is there a danger that you might ignore the conditions of
   the problem as set and therefore work out a solution
   which does not meet all the conditions?
6 Have you trained yourself to check the validity of your
   solution?

Another example is the pseudo-medical problem set out below
which creates awareness of the inhibiting effect of unchallenged and
unrecognized assumptions.

Activity 66
A Simple Medical Problem
(Disregard the likelihood of this situation existing – it is not
realistic. Your task is to solve the problem as set.)
*A patient has a deep-seated malignant condition. Unfortunately, an
operation is impossible because it is so deep-seated. The only possible
treatment is radium therapy in ray form, but the intensity of ray
required to destroy the malignant tissues is such that it will destroy
essential normal tissue, hence the treatment will kill the patient. A
young doctor is pondering on the question, aware that radium treatment
in ray form is* the only possible cure *for this case, yet, as stated
above, the potential cure is lethal. Suddenly, he exclaims, 'Why, it is
simple!' What had he recognized which allowed him to overcome the
problem?*

Students indulge in many self-defeating strategies when coping with this problem. They argue that the diagnosis was mistaken or that an operation is possible. To solve it within the
framework given above they have to discard the assumption that
the radiation has to emanate from a single source. Once this
is done, they can then see the possibility that six to eight sources

can exist. These are positioned above, below and at the sides of the patient so that the low intensity rays travel by different paths through the intervening tissues, only reaching destructive intensity as they focus on the malignancy.

This leads us to questioning our own assumptions in a very productive way. I found Peel (1960) very helpful as a source of ideas for activities on this theme. He gives a coding problem in which two letters replace a single letter. Pupils have to discard their assumption that every letter has a meaning and transfer their attention from each pair of substitute letters as a unity to the two letters separately. They then realize that the first letter has been allocated randomly, and that the second letter in each pair is the significant one. Unless the initial assumption is discarded, the code remains unbreakable.

The book by Peel is a valuable source of material, while Rokeach's (1960) Joe Doodlebug problem is a potent instrument for creating awareness of difficulties in thinking flexibly.

DEEPER ASPECTS OF COGNITIVE STYLE

It is the argument of this book that we should systematically develop the skills of study, looking back beyond techniques and skills to the underlying attitudes, defences and personality factors which shape learning. In the sixth form the tutor should help the student reflect on his learning and cognitive style. We cannot assume that this will necessarily occur in the subject area. Even if it does, we may need to help students verbalize the issues more clearly, allowing them to transfer what they know about the learning process to different contexts. A proper sense of caution must be developed in both students and teachers. The evidence is often consistent or ambiguous, therefore it would be folly to recommend one 'right' method of learning even if individuals were similar in their intellectual and temperamental needs. Equally, we must be cautious about the acceptance of extreme types such as *the converger* or *the diverger*. They are probable ideal types, formulated for the purpose of exposition, but having, by definition, no existence in reality.

Cognitive style is based on the assumption that the individual brings a particular structure or style of thinking to different curriculum areas. It is therefore a characteristic mode of functioning appearing in different contexts, although it can be modified by coercive forces within a specific situation, and also by the student's perception of what is required of him. Even so, the student has a style of attributing meaning to the learning process, and organizing facts and ideas, which to a large degree determines his success or failure.

Intolerance of ambiguity is related to, but not identical with, rigidity. It is a style of learning in which the conditional plays little part. Intellectual achievement requires the thinker to scan widely, hold disparate variables in mind, suspend judgements and perhaps see truth as conditional and propositional, certainly as subject to further revisions. The inability to accept ambiguity leads to early closure and the imposition of meaning, accompanied by a failure to take new evidence into account. The result is a very simple conceptual schema in the relevant area of learning and a lack of discriminative skills. Students whose learning is marked by the need for immediate certainty are often confused when they find contradictory viewpoints in the literature or detect a lack of consensus in the research. They then anxiously enquire which is the 'right' viewpoint. I have found it very helpful to discuss the need for tolerance of uncertainty, but there are dangers if one is not alert. Additional anxiety may be created, or the student who discovers his tendency to indulge in early closure, may feel bewildered or that too much is being asked of him. He then strengthens his existing learning patterns to avoid feeling demoralized. Therefore the tutor has to be alert to the signals of anxiety or resistance and provide some individual counselling.

Intolerance of ambiguity and vulnerability to threat cause learning to be seen as external and imposed. It is useful to build up such students' skills of analysis, the ability to appraise a position, and of reaching a balanced conclusion which is more than a reiteration of what they have said earlier. Diagrams reinforce their sense of structure, and of being in control. Without security, these students are unlikely to change.

The dogmatic personality as described by Rokeach (1960) makes very sharp distinctions between the beliefs he accepts and those he rejects. Separation allows him to indulge in undetected Orwellian double-think; he may endorse the desirability of freedom for all, for example, but also feel that certain individuals should be restricted. These incompatibles thrive in the dogmatist, who then cannot understand why his ideas are unacceptable. From our point of view, one of the causes of concern is his over-reliance on authority. More attention is paid to the credibility of the source than to content. Openness to new information is limited, but more relevant is the fact that his powers of synthesis are limited, despite the possession of analytic skills. He finds it unduly hard to integrate what he has discovered into a new whole. His pre-existing frame of reference maintains a compulsive hold in his thinking.

Exploration of the nature of authority is helpful, but the real gain comes in teaching students about the mechanisms. They then appreciate what is happening without feeling attacked or devalued.

Those intolerant of ambiguity and the dogmatist tend to be concrete thinkers and what Marton (1976) calls sign learners. Sign learners attempt to learn the key ideas off by heart. They have a regurgitative technique. For them, learning seems unproblematic because it merely consists of transferring information from the textbook or mouth of the teacher into their own notebooks, and then in due course to the examination paper. All this occurs, probably without ever entering their minds. They are honestly astonished that more is required of them.

Miller and Harvey (1973) describe the concrete thinkers and learners as holding extreme and polarized judgements, less sensitive to complex environmental areas and tending to generalize about others from incomplete information. They also possess the characteristics outlined in the description of the dogmatist.

A number of writers are producing useful ideas closely related to the problem of sixth form learning which will be of great help to the sixth form tutor. Most of this work relates to undergraduates, but this does not make it irrelevant. Sixth form teachers often express the opinion that the demands of the A-Level examination are as great as (if not greater than) those at first degree level. It is the thesis of this book that we need to anticipate difficulties in providing opportunities for intellectual development. The writers to be cited, therefore, offer important guidelines for the sixth form tutor.

Fransson (1977) argues that students adapt their learning strategies to what they believe is expected of them. His belief is that lack of interest in the subject for its own sake, test-anxiety, and over-reliance on extrinsic incentives lead to the adoption of superficial learning – rote memorization and attempts at reproducing the words of the original text. Svennson (1977) elaborates Fransson's position when he suggests that a student's perception of a situation is as important as the situation itself in understanding the relationships between the context of study and outcomes. He found a distinction between atomistic learners and holistic learners. The former seem to focus on the elements of the text in sequence rather than actively selecting the most important parts for more intensive attention. They memorize details and straight-forward information. Svennson's holistic learner attempts to understand the message as a whole, searching for the author's intention and relating the message to a wider context. If they are efficient, they reach a deeper understanding of the author's mean-ing, appearing to work within a constructive framework of appraisal. The atomistic learner's reliance on memorization leads him to accept uncritically, and mechanically reproduce what he can remember.

In this writer's work, it seems that some sixth formers approach learning in a way which leads them to apprehend quickly the deeper meanings of a text because they are sensitive to partially implicit assumptions and the purpose of the writer. Others see the text as an alien piece of material which has to be reproduced, giving undiscriminating answers to questions because they cannot see which elements are appropriate.

What does all this mean for the sixth form tutor? In assessing this, the practical constraints of time have to be kept in mind with the fact that some teachers have very limited conceptions of their teaching function. Therefore the tutor may have to explain his work to sceptical colleagues. One must also echo Fransson's warn-ing that there are no short cuts to deep level processing of informa-tion. As this book suggests, it is a long-term process beginning at entry to the secondary school – preferably earlier.

Next, we must not assume that the atomistic learner necessarily fails or does badly at A-Level. If they are of good intelligence, have been well taught and they are conscientious, they can do quite well. Difficulties probably arise later, when they are deprived of the external structure and the support provided by the school. Both tendencies – for they are such, rather than types – carry dangers. Pask (1976) shows that the holistic learner can become a 'globe trotter' who emphasizes inter-relationships and takes a broad viewpoint without supportive arguments or evidence. His serialist learner who attacks learning in strictly linear steps, build-ing up retention of details, and whose range of attention is nar-rowed to the immediate task, is in danger of 'improvidence'. He remains tied to the facts as given and does not see the implications. (Interestingly, as a trainer of experienced teachers, I suspect that the serialist is the teacher who resolutely separates theory and practice!)

What can the sixth form tutor do? First, he can bring these issues to the attention of his tutor group. Workers in this field have emphasized the importance of students' perceptions of what is needed for success. We can broaden this. We should not apologize for the fact that discussion has to be our main tool. Verbalization is essential. Without it the issues remain obscure.

Simple aids can be developed quickly by the tutor. For example, this incomplete sentence instrument may be useful in initiating a tutorial unit on styles of learning. Tutors should be aware of the defensiveness of sixth form students and their tendency to interpret concern as 'psychological rape', so the idea should be introduced carefully, and plenty of time should be allowed for the discussion to follow.

Activity 67

UNDERSTANDING YOUR STYLE OF LEARNING
Introduction
1 Maturity implies responsibility for oneself, and orientation to the future. You also want to live successfully in the present, and cope with demands for learning competently. It is helpful to analyse some of the more subtle aspects of your approach to learning.

2 Work as quickly as you can. By the way, there is no reason why you should be constrained to a single sentence. If you wish, write more.

3 What you write is for your eyes alone unless you wish to show someone. The intention is to help you clarify your perceptions and enter into a meaningful discussion.

Sentences
1 Success _____
2 I depend _____
3 Study _____
4 Teachers _____
5 Ambition _____
6 Criticism _____
7 Other students _____
8 I doubt _____
9 Parents _____
10 I expect _____
11 My difficulty _____
12 Learning is _____

Fear of exposure is often present behind a façade of composure. To prevent inhibition and face-saving, students first discuss their reactions to the instrument with a partner or in a small group of four. This leads to a better general discussion in which all have something to contribute.

We have seen that divisiveness and social anxiety are very high in some sixth form pupils. The following scale is useful, provided that the tutor has established a relationship of trust with his tutor group, and that he explains the way social and intellectual competencies are related.

Activity 68

SOCIAL SKILLS – A SIMPLE SELF ASSESSMENT FORM FOR SIXTH FORM STUDENTS

The use of this checklist

1 We all sometimes feel things go wrong for us when we are mixing with other people – perhaps we feel hurt or angry – yet there is much that we can do to prevent this happening.

2 To deal with such situations we need to be aware of the source of our social worries. This checklist can be the first step in self-understanding and dealing with the difficulty.

3 Begin by putting a tick in any of the boxes overleaf which seem to you to be IMPORTANT TO YOU in influencing your relationships with other people.

Social skills and anxieties can be seen in this way:

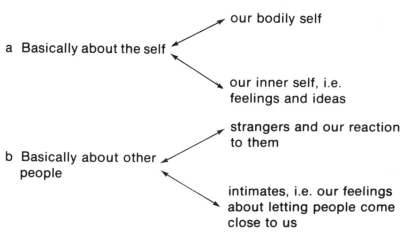

a Basically about the self

→ our bodily self

→ our inner self, i.e. feelings and ideas

b Basically about other people

→ strangers and our reaction to them

→ intimates, i.e. our feelings about letting people come close to us

How does this diagram help?

This diagram helps us make sense of what is happening to us by tracking down the sources of our difficulties. Some of us feel our bodies let us down while others feel the difficulty is within us in our feelings and fantasies. Strangers create difficulties for some of us, but for others letting people come close and really know us may be the problem.

WHERE DO YOU STAND?

THE BODILY SELF

	TOO TALL
	TOO SHORT
	FAT
	TOO THIN
	CLUMSY
	SWEATY HANDS OR FEET
	TEETH
	NOT GOOD LOOKING
	HAIR
	GLASSES
	POSTURE

THE INNER SELF

	DOUBTS ABOUT SELF
	AGGRESSIVE FEELINGS
	FEEL INADEQUATE
	SHYNESS
	GUILTY ABOUT BAD FEELINGS
	EASILY EMBARRASSED
	AFRAID THAT YOU WILL BE UNACCEPTABLE

Make any remarks about other sources of social difficulty that have not been mentioned in the two areas.

	STRANGERS	
		FEAR OF MAKING A BAD IMPRESSION
		NOT KNOWING HOW TO BEHAVE TOWARDS THEM
		DISLIKING THE LIMELIGHT
		BEING CRITICIZED
		NOT KNOWING HOW THEY WILL REACT
STRANGERS		NOT HAVING THE WORDS OR IDEAS TO TALK TO THEM
		FEELING OF BEING OUT OF ONE'S DEPTH
		INABILITY TO START A CONVERSATION
		NOT KNOWING HOW TO JOIN IN THEIR ACTIVITIES
		SAY THE WRONG THING

		NOT BEING ABLE TO TRUST THEM TO ACCEPT YOU AS YOU ARE
		NOT WANTING OTHERS TO KNOW TOO MUCH ABOUT YOU
		FEEL YOU WILL HAVE TO BE WHAT THEY WANT AND NOT YOURSELF
INTIMATE		NOT KNOWING HOW MUCH TO GIVE OR TAKE IN A CLOSE RELATIONSHIP
		FEELING THEY WILL BE DISAPPOINTED IN YOU
		FEELING YOU WILL BE DISAPPOINTED IN THEM

Make any remarks about other sources of social difficulty that have not been mentioned in the two areas.

Now comment upon what you think could be done to improve your social skills. Discuss it with someone you trust.

The follow-up would consist of a small group discussion, followed by a general discussion on the contribution of social competence to performance in the sixth form. The tutor must be very alert to any signs of anxiety. He must also acknowledge his understanding of, and show respect for, any difficulties in participation. Social anxieties *may* be associated with field dependence or undue emphasis on the form and context of learning. Witkin and Goodenough (1976) show that field dependent persons are more socially sensitive. This may be important. The field dependent person may be orientated towards reading the cues which indicate what is expected of him. Despite the speculative quality of this statement, it is very well worth discussing with sixth form groups.

Simple exercises in examining pupils' inferences were given early in this book. Variations which cause students to question their judgements can be given in the sixth form. One example is given below.

Activity 69

1 Students are presented with the following adjectives:

competent
ambitious
determined
methodical

They are then given 10 minutes to write their impression of this person.

2 Without discussion, they are then presented with the following adjectives:

warm
sensitive
imaginative
concerned

Again, they are given 10 minutes to write their impression.

3 Then they are told that all eight adjectives actually refer to the *same* person. They have 15 minutes to write their impression of the person described by all eight adjectives.

This activity, which stems from the seminal work of Asch (1952) on impression formation, is very useful. The tutor can relate it to the tendency to make assumptions and to early closure in our judgements. The discussions can lead to examination of the ways conclusions are drawn in arguments and emotive reactions to words. It may also be used to examine perceptions of the scientist and non-scientist.

Activity 70

Yet another useful activity which forms the groundwork for discussion of over-reliance on the credibility of source can be taken from social psychology. In this the tutor has prepared a statement on violence in modern society. All the tutor group have the same statement but it is attributed to different sources in the introductory paragraph. To ensure comparability the main statement is photocopied, while the introductory paragraph is stapled to it as a separate sheet. A more effective way, if facilities are available, is to type the introductory paragraph separately, placing it above the main statement when photocopying. The introductory paragraph is then changed as necessary.

The statement could be attributed to:

a a high court judge;

b a retired colonel from Tunbridge Wells;

c a pop star;

d a social worker.

The tutor asks students to rate their:

a strength of agreement or disagreement with the viewpoint;

b assessment of the reliability of the statement.

Students are not allowed to communicate with each other.

A quick blackboard summary of the results is built up. This is simple because each sheet has an appropriate letter A to D at the bottom left-hand corner. The tutor moves the discussion gradually to our reliance upon authority. On several occasions, as a follow-up, I have asked two students to read Milgram (1974) on obedience to authority. They then presented a taped summary to the tutor group with which I was working. The questions of belief in expert power, and trust in authority, led to examination of personal tendencies in using evidence. The tutor will find it possible to extend the discussion in very productive ways.

Activity 71

Self-evaluation of the work of the student has to be stimulated. In some of our early work on sixth form study skills we found that students were mark hungry. This led them to concentrate on the mark, and ignore the careful comments made by the teacher. Evaluation of the student's own work leads, I find, to a growing appreciation of the usefulness of the subject specialist's remarks.

Additionally, a simple self-evaluation sheet of the kind set out below is one step in the move towards holistic learning. (Both holistic and linear learning may be necessary, the good student knowing which is applicable to a particular task.) The schedule bridges the gap between theory and practice in a practical manner if the tutor makes the preliminary diagram the subject of a tutorial period.

A SELF-ASSESSMENT SCHEDULE FOR SIXTH FORM STUDENTS
The purpose of the schedule

1 An important skill required in commerce, industry, university and other forms of higher education is that of constructively criticizing your own performance. This means that you have to

learn to examine your work in ways which suggest the steps you can take to improve it. *If you honestly desire success then you will act on your suggestions.*

2 The attempt at self-assessment will be even more productive if you work with a friend taking the same subject. Mutual support coupled with constructive criticism can lead to the development of productive strategies resulting in a higher level of achievement.

3 The capacity to evaluate their own work is a feature of those who achieve highly and attain success in their chosen fields. You may care to discuss this, noting the relationship to maturity of the factors brought out in the diagram below.

THE POOR PERFORMER IN THE SIXTH FORM.	THE HIGH ACHIEVER WHO USES HIS POTENTIAL IN THE SIXTH FORM.
1 Relies on external controls, especially rewards and sanctions from parents and teachers.	1 Derives rewards from meeting his self-set high standards of performance.
2 Depends solely upon the comments of his teachers for evaluation of his work.	2 Has commitment to his subject and *actively searches* for ways of achieving his standard of excellence.
3 Works *almost entirely* to satisfy the demands of his parents, teachers and examiners.	3 Sees the relevance of his subjects to his plans for the future.
4 Fundamentally believes that luck or chance determine his fate in life.	4 Accepts the responsibility for both his successes and failures.
5 Blames others for his failures, inadequacies and difficulties.	5 Will persevere in the face of difficulty, but examines the situation to see if his methods of study need to be modified.
6 Relies on authority figures to set his goals.	6 Tries to experiment with method of study and problem solving in a responsible manner.
7 Tends to reproduce the ideas of others in an uncritical way.	

Your use of this schedule

1 You can use it in many ways. Responsibility for using a tool such as this schedule is always given to you. It must serve your purposes. *It should not be used to assess every piece of work for that would either be obsessional or operate to destroy the impact of the schedule.*

2 You could decide to:
  a apply it to every sixth piece of work;
  b confine its use to one of your subjects;
  c use it as a basis for discussion with your subject teacher or sixth form tutor.
3 Whatever your use of the schedule you should:
  a be able to justify your choice of procedure in a logical way *to yourself* – it is your life!
  b be consistent – self-assessment and its use in improving performance is a skill which comes with time.

Assessment schedule
Please make your comments in each box.

---

1 *Layout and presentation*
This is not trivial, it is part of the process of becoming competent. It is both attractive and clear. Does the presentation convey to the reader the effort you put into the assignment? Does it reflect an image of efficiency?

---

2 *The structure and clarity*
This is as important to scientists as it is to the arts student. Scientists must communicate with clarity and precision. Was the assignment broken down into sections? Did you introduce your ideas or results clearly? Did you end with a clear conclusion which incorporated an assessment of the evidence or of the validity and strength of your arguments? Did you plan the structure by constructing a flow diagram or logical framework?

3 *Preparation and planning*
Once you have undertaken some evaluation of the end product you are in a position to assess the effectiveness of your
preparation. Did you give sufficient care to planning the way in
which you tackled the task? Did you examine the question or
task carefully, relating it to previous work? You should try to
see the importance of an assignment to the whole topic.

4 *Quality of thought and argument*
You may find it thought-provoking to ask if you:
– carefully appraised the evidence or arguments throughout
  the period of preparation as well as when you were producing
  the final product;
– have the habit of scanning the evidence to ensure that
  everything relevant was taken into account;
– tried to detect weaknesses and ambiguities in your thinking
  and deal with them.
Make comments on these points below:

5 *Anticipate your teacher's comments*
(Don't forget to check the accuracy of your prediction!)

6 *Changes in the approach*
If you could begin again what changes would you make in the:

a way you tackled the assignment?

b content and structure of the piece of work?

7 *Using the analysis*
Now make *two* or *three* points that you will apply to your work immediately.

In the first term of the sixth form students tend to miss the structure of the homework timetable. The old complaint, 'I mean to get started, but somehow I don't', arises again. The tutor may begin by discussing the reasons for procrastination, and the conditions for effective working. These differ from individual to individual: we must not assume that a background of pop music is necessarily distracting, or leads to ineffective study. Anxious, extrovert and restless students often need it as a prerequisite for study.

The tutor can alert students to the importance of planning 24 hours in advance. The weekly diary given below is self-explanatory, although the tutor should introduce it through elaboration of the points above. There is little point in reproducing the whole diary, therefore the first two days only are given.

STUDY SKILLS: ORGANIZATION AND EVALUATION OF PRIVATE STUDY

A WEEKLY DIARY

Notes

1 Planning the way you use your time for private study raises your productivity and puts you in charge of your learning. There is little point in working for long periods of time in a haphazard way. That is the surest way of producing frustration, boredom and the sense of not being in control.

2 There are three sections for each day's entries in the weekly diary:

a In the left-hand section enter details of what you intend to do. *Be precise.* Don't write 'History' or 'Mathematics', state *exactly* what you are going to do, e.g.:

History – the guilds – concept of the *'Just price'* – implications for organization.

b The next section draws your attention to the amount of time you allocate to testing yourself, raising questions and *actively organizing* what you have learned. *This is fundamental.* The nearer you are to an examination, the more time you should spend on this. This aspect of study can involve:

– testing yourself on recall – you *can* record your answers and then play them back as a check;

– formulating, and then answering a question;

– rewriting the notes you have taken in your *own* words;

– constructing a diagram – either a pattern or a logical 'step-by-step' flow diagram.

c The right-hand section is based on the assumption that as an intelligent person striving for success you are the best critic of your private study methods. It is your future and the responsibility belongs to you. Make comments immediately. They should be practical – e.g.:

– 'must give myself more time for checking what I have learned';

– 'wasted time – must read the question more carefully'.

3 As an active learner you must decide how *long* you study and the *time* of day you perform best. Each one of us is different; therefore these have to be personal decisions. You should not, however, usually study for long periods without short breaks. The length of each period is a matter for you. Indeed, you may find it best to study without a break. In the end, you have to make your own decisions.

	Precise details	Time given to testing and recall	Comments
SUNDAY			
MONDAY			

Follow-up discussion could centre upon the physical conditions for learning – sound, light, company, temperature – and the way they impinge differently on individuals.

Fear of success

The ambivalences described at the beginning of this chapter have been a matter of concern for the writer during the past eleven years. Provision of the mechanics of study skills does little to modify these deeper influences on achievement. Positive expectations of others assume a compulsive character, becoming a source of threat. Some individuals secretly doubt the legitimacy of their own wishes and expectations. Occasionally one meets a student who seems to desire success, yet appears to court failure assiduously.

Work with these students suggested that they had conflicts and uncertainties associated with their desire for independence. Often the tensions seemed stronger when the student's family seemed in a marginal position in the local community because of social background, ethnic origins and values. The family had also created a symbolic environment in which success and achievement played an all-important part.

It seemed important to offer such students personal counselling. Discussion of this is beyond the scope of this book, but it is useful to examine more generally feelings about success. The topic can be opened up by discussion of the following:

1 What is the meaning of success to you?

2　What kind of person is successful in examinations?
3　What costs do you feel are attached to being successful?

It seems useful for the tutor to help students explore their fears about accepting the responsibilities that success brings. In discussions, there are overtones of sibling rivalry, and the fear of jealousy, in some individuals. An inner insecurity makes them vulnerable to the destructive comments – often existing in anticipation only – of their peers. Both sexes seem to fear the comments of their own sex more than those of the opposite sex. The old proverb, 'Pride comes before a fall', can be revised to read, 'Success brings the danger of a fall, therefore is it worth it?'

These tendencies are strong in only a few students, but the occasional doubt or feelings of wishing to avoid success come to many sixth form students. Methods of coping with such reactions seem to merit a place in the tutorial work. Perhaps it is not without significance that those students who react most apprehensively to the responsibilities of success seem to lack real commitment to their subject disciplines. Our task is to reduce the sense of threat by helping them face it squarely.

Author's note
In this discussion of study skills at sixth form level I have tried to avoid repeating what I have written elsewhere. The tutor is therefore also advised to consult the relevant chapter in *The Teacher and Pastoral Care* (Hamblin, 1978).

Epilogue

Simultaneously found wanting and yet untried! This is the fate of pastoral care. What has been described as pastoral care in some schools has been an amorphous, uncoordinated and low level form of 'emotional first aid' or an imprecise attempt to 'get to know them'. In this book it has been argued that the tutor makes a real contribution to raising the level of performance of those for whose well-being he is responsible.

My task has, however, been a limited one: to illustrate the way in which tutorial periods can be used to enrich the pupil's style of learning. Study skills are merely one part of the guidance programme. Equally relevant is the fact that the pastoral effort alone cannot compensate for a poorly designed curriculum, ineffective teaching methods and poor organization. What I have tried to provide is a number of starting points and ideas. Had I attempted to impose a uniform pattern on schools, not only would I have been in the position of denying the fact that each secondary school is a unique social system with its own input, transformation processes and conception of output, but I would have been guilty of crass pretensions to omnipotence. This does not mean one is reduced to impotence, however. The basic issues have been isolated, and many ideas, based on experience, have been shared.

Yet it is possible for these activities to be misused or reduced to sterility. The responsibility therefore lies with the deputy head in charge of pastoral care to see that heads of year or house have the opportunity to explore the issues behind skills in some depth. They, in turn, must be prepared to exercise an educative function, and provide their team of tutors with purposeful leadership.

I have given of what I have, realizing that it may be insufficient. Yet I believe that even in this age when we as teachers feel insecure, and threatened, the activities described can be the points of departure for exciting journeys into learning. Perhaps we can end by reminding ourselves of the words of Robert South:

'It is idleness that creates impossibilities; and, where men care not to do a thing, they shelter themselves under a persuasion that it cannot be done. The shortest and surest way to prove a work possible is strenuously to set about it.'

References

Adams, J., Hayes, J. and Hopson, B. (1976) *Transition: Understanding and Managing Personal Change*, London: Robertson.

Ahier, P. (1978) *An Experimental Study of Adolescent Girls who Absent Themselves from School*, Unpublished P.C.G.C. Dissertation, University College of Swansea.

Alexander, W. and Burke, W. (1972) Independent study in secondary schools, *Interchange, Vol. 3.*, Nos. 2 and 3, pp. 102–113.

Allport, G. (1935) Attitudes. In Murchison, C. (Ed) *Handbook of Social Psychology*, Worcester, Mass.: Clark University Press.

Allport, G. and Postman, L. (1945) The Basic Psychology of Rumour, *Transactions of the New York Academy of Sciences*, Series II, *VIII.*, pp. 61–81.

Atkinson, J. and Feather, N. (1966) *A Theory of Achievement Motivation*, New York: Wiley.

Atkinson, J. and Raynor, J. (1974) *Motivation and Achievement*, Washington, D.C.: Winston.

Ausubel, D. (1968) *Educational Psychology*, New York: Holt, Rinehart and Winston.

Banks, O. and Finlayson, D. (1973) *Success and Failure in the Secondary School*, London: Methuen.

Bartlett, F. (1932) *Remembering*, Cambridge: Cambridge University Press.

Beaumont, G. (1976) *A Comparison of the Effect of Behavioural Counselling and Teacher Support on the Attendance of Truants*, Unpublished Diploma in School Counselling Dissertation, University College of Swansea.

Bennett, N. (1976) *Teaching Styles and Pupil Progress*, London: Open Books.

Birney, R., Burdick, H. and Teevan, R. (1969) *Fear of Failure Motivation*, New York: Wiley.

Bloom, B. (1976) *Human Characteristics and School Learning*, New York: McGraw-Hill.

Byrne, D. (1964) Repression – Sensitization as a Dimension of Personality, In Maher, B. (Ed) *Progress in Experimental Personality Research*, Vol. 1, New York: Academic Press.

Cooper, D. (1971) *The Death of the Family*, London: Allen and Unwin.

Covington, M. and Beery, R. (1976) *Self-Worth and School Learning*, New York: Holt, Rinehart and Winston.

Dean, J. (1978) *Report from the Sixteen Plus Education Unit*, Windsor: N.F.E.R.

Erikson, E. (1968) *Identity, Youth and Crisis*, London: Faber and Faber.

Fishbein, M. (1967) Attitude and the Prediction of Behaviour, *Readings in Attitude Theory and Measurement*, New York: Wiley.

Ford, J. (1969) *Social Class and the Comprehensive School*, London: Routledge and Kegan Paul.

Fransson, A. (1977) Intrinsic Motivation – Extrinsic Motivation, *British Journal of Educational Psychology*, 47, pp. 244–257.

Gaudry, E. and Spielberger, C. (1971) *Anxiety and Educational Achievement*, Sydney: Wiley.

Goodman, G. (1972) *Companionship Therapy*, San Francisco: Jossey-Bass.

Guerney, B. (Ed) (1969) *Psychotherapeutic Agents*, New York: Holt, Rinehart and Winston.

Hamblin, D. (1974) *The Teacher and Counselling*, Oxford: Blackwell.

Hamblin, D. (1978) *The Teacher and Pastoral Care*, Oxford: Blackwell.

Heider, F. and Simmel, M. (1944) An Experimental Study of Apparent Behaviour, *American Journal of Psychology* 57, pp. 243–259.

Jacobs, V. (1974) *A Study of the Effects of Counselling on Pupils Experiencing Difficulties with A-Level Work*, Unpublished Diploma in School Counselling dissertation, University College of Swansea.

Jones, E. and Gerard, H. (1967) *Foundations of Social Psychology*, New York: Wiley.

Kandel, D. and Lesser, G. (1972) *Youth in Two Worlds*, San Francisco: Jossey–Bass.

Katz, D. (1960) 'The Functional Approach to the Study of Attitudes', *Public Opinion Quarterly*, 24, pp. 163–204.

Katz, P. and Zigler, E. (1967) Self-image Disparity: A Developmental Approach, *Journal of Personality and Social Psychology* 5, pp. 186–195.

Kelly, G. (1955) *The Psychology of Personal Constructs*, New York: Norton.

Krech, D., Crutchfield, R. and Ballachey, E. (1962) *Individual in Society*, New York: McGraw-Hill.

Lazarus, R. (1966) *Psychological Stress and the Coping Process*, New York: McGraw-Hill.

Lazarus, R. (1969) *Patterns of Adjustment and Human Effectiveness*, New York: McGraw-Hill.

Leach, P. (1965) *Social and Perceptual Inflexibility in School Children in Relation to Maternal Child-Rearing Habits*. Unpublished Ph.D. Thesis, London School of Economics, University of London.

Lewin, K. (1935) *A Dynamic Theory of Personality*, New York: McGraw-Hill.

Mandler, G. and Sarason, S. (1952) 'A study of anxiety and learning', *Journal of Abnormal and Social Psychology* 47, pp. 166–173.

Marton, F. (1976) 'What Does it Take to Learn?' In Entwistle, N. (Ed) *Strategies for Research and Development in Higher Education*, Amsterdam: Swets and Zeitlinger.

Marton, F. and Säljö, R. (1976) On Qualitative Differences in Learning – Outcome and Process, *British Journal of Educational Psychology*, 46, pp. 4–11.

McClelland, D., Atkinson, J., Clark, R. and Lowell, E. (1953) *The Achievement Motive*, New York: Appleton–Century–Croft.

McGuire, W. (1969) In Lindzey, G. and Aronson, E. *Handbook of Social Psychology*, *Vol. 3*, Reading, Mass.: Addison-Wesley.

Messick, S. *et al.* (1976) *Individuality in Learning*, San Francisco: Jossey–Bass.

Michotte, A. (1954) *La Perception de la Causalité* (2nd Edn), Louvain: Publications Universitaires de Louvain.

Milgram, S. (1974) *Obedience to Authority*, London: Tavistock.

Miller, H. and Harvey, C. (1973) Effects of Concreteness–Abstractness and Anxiety on Intellectual and Motor Performance, *Journal of Counselling and Clinical Psychology*, *40*, pp. 444–451.

Naylor, F. (1972) *Personality and Educational Achievement*, Sydney: Wiley.

Oppenheim, A. (1966) *Questionnaire Design and Attitude Measurement*, London: Heinemann.

O'Shea, M. (1980) *A Study of Students' Attitudes to Public Examinations in Irish Secondary Schools*, Unpublished M.Ed. Dissertation, Swansea: University College of Swansea.

Parker, J. and Rubin, L. (1966) *Process as Content: Curriculum Design and the Application of Knowledge*, Chicago: Rand McNally.

Pask, G. (1976) Styles and Strategies of Thinking, *British Journal of Educational Psychology*, *46*, pp. 128–148.

Patty, R. and Safford, S. (1977) Motive to Avoid Success, Motive to Avoid Failure, State-Trait Anxiety and Performance, In Spielberger, C. and Sarason, I. (Eds) *Stress and Anxiety, Vol. 4*, New York: Wiley.

Peel, E. (1960) *The Pupil's Thinking*, London: Oldbourne.

Phares, E. (1976) *Locus of Control in Personality*, Morristown, N.J.: General Learning Press.

Phillips, B. (1978) *School Stress and Anxiety*, New York: Human Sciences Press.

Robinson, F. (1970) *Effective Study*, New York: Harper and Row (4th Edition).

Rokeach, M. (1960) *The Open and Closed Mind*, New York: Basic Books.

Rosenberg, J. (1965) *Society and the Adolescent Self-Image*, Princeton: Princeton University Press.

Rotter, J. (1966) Generalized Expectancies for Internal versus External Control of Reinforcement, *Psychological Monographs, Vol. 80*, No. 1 (Whole No. 609).

Rotter, J., Chance, J. and Phares, E. (1972) *Applications of a Social Learning Theory of Personality*, New York: Holt, Rinehart and Winston.

Rowntree, E. (1970) *Learn How to Study*, London: MacDonald.

Rutter, M., Maughan, B., Mortimore, P. and Ouston, J. (1979) *Fifteen Thousand Hours*, London: Open Books.

Sarason, S., Davidson, K., Lighthall, F. and Waite, R. (1958) A test anxiety scale for children, *Child Development*, *29*, pp. 105–113.

Secord, P. and Backman, C. (1964) *Social Psychology*, New York: McGraw-Hill.

Skinner, B. (1971) *Beyond Freedom and Dignity*, New York: Knopf.

Spielberger, C. and Sarason, S. (Eds) (1976) *Stress and Anxiety*, Washington: Hemisphere.

Spielberger, C. and Weitz, H. (1964) Improving the Academic Performance of College Freshmen: A Group–Counselling Approach to the Prevention of Under-Achievement, *Psychological Monograph, 78*, No. 13 (Whole No. 590).

Sumner, R. and Warburton, F. (1972) *Achievement in Secondary School*, Slough: N.F.E.R.

Svensson, L. (1977) On Qualitative Differences in Learning, *British Journal of Educational Psychology, 47*, pp. 233–243.

Thomas, J. (1973) *Self Concept in Psychology and Education*, London: N.F.E.R.

Thoresen, C. and Mahoney, M. (1974) *Behavioral Self-Control*, New York: Holt, Rinehart and Winston.

Vorrath, H. and Brendtro, L. (1974) *Positive Peer Culture*, Chicago: Aldine.

Watson, D. and Tharp, R. (1972) *Self-Directed Behaviour: Self-Modification for Personal Adjustment*, Monterey, Calif.: Brooks/Cole.

White, R. (1959) Motivation reconsidered: the Concept of Competence, *Psychological Review, 66*, pp. 297–333.

Williams, M. (1979) The Sixth Form Common Room as an Arena, *Educational Review, 31*, No. 3, pp. 193–203.

Witkin, H. and Goodenough, D. (1976) *Field Dependence and Interpersonal Behaviour*, ETS RB-76-12 Princeton: Educational Testing Service.

Wylie, R. (1961) *The Self Concept*, Nebraska: University of Nebraska Press.

Yinger, J., Ikeda, I., Laycock, F. and Cutler, S. (1977) *Middle Start: An Experiment in the Educational Enrichment of Young Adolescents*, Cambridge: Cambridge University Press.

Youngman, M. (1978) Six Reactions to School Transfer, *British Journal of Educational Psychology, 48*, pp. 280–284.

Index